Presented To:

Blake Truitt

From:

Bill, Carrie, James, Jacob & Tucker

Date:

May 26, 2001

Blake,

In Psalm 139, God
tells you of His love for
you. We pray you will know
His love and the plans He has for
your life. Jeremiah 29:11
God bless & keep you!

Love
Bill + Carrie
+ boys

God's Little Devotional Book
FOR THE
CLASS OF 2001

Honor Books
Tulsa, Oklahoma

God's Little Devotional Book for the Class of 2001
ISBN 1-56292-949-6
Copyright © 2001 by Honor Books
P.O. Box 55388
Tulsa, Oklahoma 74155

God's Little Devotional Book
FOR THE
CLASS OF 2001

INTRODUCTION

Congratulations! As a member of the Class of 2001, you are graduating into a world poised to set the pace for a promising new millennium. Breathtaking technologies are drawing us closer to a global community. We are flooded with information, bombarded by choices, and staggered by moral dilemmas our parents and grandparents never imagined. It is a world filled to the brim with possibilities and challenges.

So how can you make good choices for your life in this bold, new world? How can you cut through the hype and find the answers you need to build a productive and fulfilling life for yourself?

In *God's Little Devotional Book for the Class of 2001,* you will find insight and wisdom fit for a new millennium. The timeless truths presented in these pages will help you anchor your life on solid rock and give you the edge you need to be successful in our brave, new world.

THE WORLD WANTS YOUR BEST, BUT GOD WANTS YOUR ALL.

Thou shalt love the Lord thy God with all thy heart,
and with all thy soul, and with all thy mind.
Matthew 22:37

For months Eric Liddell trained with his heart set on winning the 100-meter race at the Olympics of 1924. Many sportswriters predicted he would win. At the games, however, Liddell learned that the 100-meter race was scheduled to be run on a Sunday. This posed a major problem for him, because Liddell did not believe he could honor God by running on the Lord's Day. He bowed out of the race and his fans were stunned. Some who had praised him in the past now called him a fool. He came under intense pressure to change his mind, but Liddell stood firm.

Then a runner dropped out of the 400-meter race, which was scheduled on a weekday, and Liddell offered to fill the slot. This was not really "his race"—the distance was four times as long as the race for which he had trained diligently. Even so, Liddell crossed the tape as victor and set a record of 47.6 seconds in the process. He had earned an Olympic gold medal . . . *and* made an uncompromising stand for his faith.

Liddell went on to become a missionary in China, where he died in a war camp in 1945. He lives in history as a man known more for his inner mettle than for his gold medal.

THE BEST THING ABOUT THE FUTURE IS THAT IT COMES ONLY ONE DAY AT A TIME.

"Don't be anxious about tomorrow.
God will take care of your tomorrow too.
Live one day at a time."
Matthew 6:34 TLB

Warmiwañusca, aptly translated "Dead Woman's Pass," loomed in front of Debra like an impenetrable fortress. The pass rose 13,750 feet—seemingly straight up. Debra longed for a switchback, or better yet, a 7-11. Halfway up, she had her first bout with altitude sickness. But there was no way she'd turn back.

Her guide suggested she try the Peruvian "Walk of the Patient One." "Take one step only one inch ahead of your last," he explained. "Don't try to keep up with the others. Go at the pace God designed you for."

Debra not only reached the top but finished the four-day trek over Peru's Inca Trail. The forty-year-old mother of two fulfilled a dream she'd had since she was twelve. "If I'd known what the path was going to be like, I never would have gone," she said. "I would've thought I'd never make it. And I would have missed the greatest adventure of my life."

Graduation is a time of great expectations and adventures. But in His wisdom, God only let's you see as far ahead as today. When life's rough mountain peaks and deep valleys stand in the way of your goals, don't be discouraged. Take your eyes off those around you. Take a fresh look at the person God designed you to be. Then continue toward your destination, one step at a time.

SHOOT FOR THE MOON. EVEN IF YOU MISS IT YOU WILL LAND AMONG THE STARS.

Aim for perfection.
2 Corinthians 13:11 NIV

A young man sat in a park watching squirrels scamper among the trees. He was feeling confused about his future and wondering which direction to take with his life, when he noticed a squirrel jumping from one high tree to another. It appeared to be aiming for a limb so far out of reach that the leap looked like suicide. As the young man had anticipated, the squirrel missed its mark, but it landed, safe and unconcerned, on a branch several feet lower. Then it climbed to its goal, and all was well.

An old man sitting on the other end of the bench remarked, "Funny, I've seen hundreds of 'em jump like that, especially when there are dogs all around and they can't come down to the ground. A lot of 'em miss, but I've never seen one get hurt tryin'." Then he chuckled and added, "I guess them squirrels must figure it's better to take a risk than to spend their whole life in one tree."

The young man thought, *A squirrel takes a chance. Do I have less nerve than a squirrel?* He made up his mind in that moment to take the risk he had been thinking about. Sure enough, he landed safely, in a position higher than he had even dared to imagine.

What dream are you aiming for? Does it seem out of reach? Take a leap of faith. God will always catch you if you fall.

THE MAN WHO WINS MAY HAVE BEEN COUNTED OUT SEVERAL TIMES, BUT HE DIDN'T HEAR THE REFEREE.

Though a righteous man falls
seven times, he rises again.
Proverbs 24:16 NIV

14

The difference between success and failure is often the ability to get up just one more time than you fall down! Consider the lives of these Bible characters:

- Moses easily could have given up. He had an "interrupted" childhood and lived with a foster family. He also had a strong temper, a stammering tongue, and a criminal record, but when God called him, he said "yes."

- Joshua had seen the Promised Land, but he was not allowed to enter. Instead, he was forced to wander in the wilderness for forty years with cowards who didn't believe, as he did, that they could conquer their enemies and possess the land. He could have given up in discouragement, but he held on to God's promises.

- Peter did not have a smooth transition from fisherman to apostle. He sank while trying to walk on water, was strongly rebuked by Jesus for trying to tell Him what to do, and denied knowing Jesus when Jesus needed him most. He easily could have seen himself as a hopeless failure. But when the opportunity came to preach the message of God's love before thousands on the Day of Pentecost, he was ready and willing

No matter what you've done, what mistakes you've made, what errors you may have committed, you're not a failure until you lay down and quit.

15

THE SECRET OF SUCCESS IS TO DO THE COMMON THINGS UNCOMMONLY WELL.

Seest thou a man diligent in his business?
he shall stand before kings;
he shall not stand before mean men.
Proverbs 22:29

CLASS OF 2001

Helping the deaf to communicate was Alexander Graham Bell's motivation for his life's work, perhaps because his mother and wife were both deaf. "If I can make a deaf-mute talk," Bell said, "I can make metal talk." For five frustrating and impoverished years, he experimented with a variety of materials in an effort to make a metal disk that, vibrating in response to sound, could reproduce those sounds and send them over an electrified wire.

During a visit to Washington D.C., he called on Joseph Henry, a scientist who was a pioneer in research related to electricity. He presented his ideas to him and asked his advice: Should he let someone else perfect the telephone or should he do it himself? Henry encouraged him to do it himself, even though Bell complained that he lacked the necessary knowledge of electricity. Henry's brief solution was, "If you don't have it, get it."

So Bell studied electricity. A year later, while obtaining a patent for the telephone, the officials in the patent office credited him with knowing more about electricity than all the other inventors of his day combined.

Hard work. Study. Hope. Persistence. These are all "common things." They are also the keys to doing uncommonly well.

CLASS OF 2001

17

BLESSED IS THE MAN WHO FINDS OUT WHICH WAY GOD IS MOVING AND THEN GETS GOING IN THE SAME DIRECTION.

Whether you turn to the right or to the left,
your ears will hear a voice behind you, saying,
"This is the way; walk in it."
Isaiah 30:21 NIV

"Okay, God," prayed Becky. "This afternoon is set aside for you. I'm taking the next two hours just to pray." Becky had never talked to God that long before. Feeling that it might become difficult to stay with it, she wrote out an extensive list of people and problems she felt she needed to pray about.

Soon after she started, Becky felt that she should give her friend Teri a call. She'd wanted to invite Teri and her family over to lunch, but had never quite gotten around to asking them. Fearing that her mind was starting to wander, Becky tried to go back to her list. But Teri kept coming to mind. After several attempts to get her mind back on what she was doing, Becky gave up and phoned Teri.

As Becky began to voice her invitation, Teri started laughing. Taken aback, Becky wondered what great social blunder she had just committed. But Teri explained, "Just five minutes ago, I was having a regular pity party, crying because no one at our church ever invites us over. I had just said those very words to my husband when the phone rang."

Are you willing to let God change your agenda? His timing is always perfect. Today when you pray, be sure to listen for God's voice speaking to your heart even as you verbalize your concerns to Him. Why settle for a monologue when you can enjoy a two-way conversation.

CLASS OF 2001

19

NEVER THINK THAT GOD'S DELAYS ARE GOD'S DENIALS. HOLD ON; HOLD FAST; HOLD OUT. PATIENCE IS GENIUS.

Whenever you face trials of any kind, consider it nothing but joy, because you know that the testing of your faith produces endurance.
James 1:2-3 NRSV

Theodor was an artist, of sorts. He drew cartoons for a "creature-of-the-month" ad campaign for a popular insecticide called "Flit." But Theodor wanted to expand the scope of his commercial illustrating. Unfortunately, his advertising contract wouldn't allow it. So instead, he decided to try his hand at writing and illustrating children's books.

After twenty-seven rejections of his first attempt, *A Story No One Can Beat,* Theodor was ready to give up. On his way home to burn his manuscript, Theodor ran into an old schoolmate who had just been hired as a children's book editor at Vanguard Press. With a change of the title to *And To Think It Began on Mulberry Street,* Theodor's first book finally made it to press.

Thus began the career of the best-selling children's author of all time, Theodor Seuss Geisel. In addition to winning the Pulitzer Prize for fiction in 1984, "Dr. Seuss" was also awarded eight honorary degrees. When he died at the age of eighty-seven, Theodor's books had sold more than 200 million copies, and he was receiving nearly 1,500 fan letters a week.[1]

How soon is too soon to give up? It is any time before you're absolutely certain God wants you to head in a new direction. After all, who knows what unexpected rewards the second try, the tenth, or the twenty-seventh will hold?

NO HORSE GETS
ANYWHERE UNTIL
HE IS HARNESSED.
NO LIFE EVER GROWS
GREAT UNTIL IT IS
FOCUSED, DEDICATED,
DISCIPLINED.

*In a race, everyone runs but only one person
gets first prize. . . . To win the contest
you must deny yourselves many things
that would keep you from doing your best.*
1 Corinthians 9:24-25 TLB

Charles Oakley, forward for the New York Knicks and an NBA All-star, has a reputation for being one of basketball's best rebounders. It's his toughness, however, that has probably contributed the most to his outstanding sports career.

While other professional players seem to have frequent injuries or are sidelined for other reasons, Oakley has had very few injuries over the course of his thirteen-year career, even though he has absorbed a great deal of physical punishment on the court. He is often pushed and fouled. He puts in miles each game, running up and down the court. He frequently dives into the stands for loose balls, to the extent that the courtside media teases him about being a working hazard. According to Oakley, his tenacity and energy were instilled in him by his grandfather, Julius Moss.

Moss was a farmer in Alabama who did most of his field work by hand. "Other people had more equipment than he did," Oakley says. "He didn't have a tractor, but he got the work done. No excuses." Moss, who died in 1990, developed all sorts of aches and pains in his life, but he laughed at them and went about his business. Oakley saw a lesson in that— nothing should prevent him from earning a day's pay.

Being focused, dedicated, and disciplined will make the difference between a mediocre life and a *great* life.

NOTHING GREAT WAS EVER ACHIEVED WITHOUT ENTHUSIASM.

The joy of the LORD is your strength.
Nehemiah 8:10

After years of working in Rome on life-sized sculptures, Michelangelo went to Florence, where a large block of splendid white Carrara marble had been obtained for a colossal statue. Within weeks, he had signed an agreement to complete a rendition of David for the cathedral.

Contract in hand, he started in at once, working with a furious energy so great that he often slept in his clothes, resenting the time it took to take them off and put them on again. He faultlessly examined and precisely measured the marble to see what pose it could accommodate. He made sketches of possible attitudes and careful, detailed drawings from models. He tested his ideas in wax on a small scale. When he was finally satisfied with his design, only then did he pick up a chisel and mallet.

Michelangelo approached painting the ceiling of the Sistine Chapel with the same intensity. Lying at uncomfortable angles on hard boards, while breathing the suffocating air just under the vault, Michelangelo suffered with inflamed eyes and irritated skin from the plaster dust. And for the next four years, he was literally sweating in physical distress as he worked.

If you aren't passionate about the work you do, find something about which you can become enthused. You may not be in a position to change jobs, but you can always find a hobby, develop a talent, or hone a skill. Such pursuits can greatly increase the joy of living.

CLASS OF 2001

25

THE WORLD IS GOVERNED MORE BY APPEARANCES THAN REALITIES.

*These are a shadow of the things
that were to come; the reality,
however, is found in Christ.*
Colossians 2:17 NIV

CLASS OF
2001

A story is told about the chance meeting of Pablo Picasso and an American soldier. The two of them were seated at a Parisian café and decided to share a drink or two. It wasn't surprising that their conversation soon turned to art. So Picasso tried to explain to the soldier the style of art for which he was known.

"I just don't like modern art," remarked the soldier.

When Picasso asked him why not, the soldier said that modern art was not realistic. He said that he preferred paintings that actually looked like the things they were supposed to be paintings of.

Picasso said nothing. To break the uncomfortable silence, the soldier decided to share a few photos from his wallet of his girlfriend back in the States. Picasso looked at each of the photos politely. Then holding one of the photos in his hand, he commented to the soldier, "Goodness! Is she really this small?"[2]

Every situation in your life can be seen from a variety of angles, each presenting a different point of view. But there is only one true reality—life seen from God's point of view. There is a bigger picture, an eternal one, hidden behind the canvas of every ordinary day. Even though you can't always see it, it is there.

DO ALL THE GOOD
YOU CAN TO ALL
THE PEOPLE YOU
CAN, IN ALL THE
WAYS YOU CAN,
AS OFTEN AS EVER
YOU CAN, AS LONG
AS YOU CAN.

*Do not forget to do good and to share with
others, for with such sacrifices God is pleased.*
Hebrews 13:16 NIV

28

CLASS OF
2001

The restaurant was almost empty. Still, the waiter seated Lisa and her grandmother right next to a single businessman, who was enjoying his newspaper and a leisurely lunch. Lisa began to panic. She was accustomed to her grandmother's idiosyncrasies since the onset of Alzheimer's, but she wasn't sure the businessman would be as understanding.

As soon as they were seated, the questions began. "How am I going to pay for this food? I don't have any money. Who's paying my bills? I shouldn't have moved here. I'm just a burden. Why don't you leave me in the gutter to die?"

Patiently, Lisa tried to calm her grandmother's fears, answering the same questions she answered week after week. Forty minutes passed. Lisa couldn't stop worrying about the man sitting next to them. *He's trying to relax,* she thought. *My grandmother's probably driving him crazy.*

Lisa was relieved when the man finally folded his paper and prepared to leave. Then to her surprise, he headed straight for their table. Lisa prepared to apologize for any aggravation her grandmother might have caused him. Instead, he looked at Lisa with a smile and whispered, "When I get older, I hope I have a granddaughter just like you."

Even the smallest gesture of kindness can make a big difference in someone's life. Keep your eyes and heart open for the opportunities today brings.

IF YOU CAN'T CHANGE YOUR CIRCUMSTANCES, CHANGE THE WAY YOU RESPOND TO THEM.

*We know that in all things God
works for the good of those who love him,
who have been called according to his purpose.*
Romans 8:28 NIV

None of the kids on the block knew why Mrs. Greer was so mean. All they knew for sure was that she hated kids. If a ball rolled into her yard, they forgot it. After knocking on her door once, no one ever tried it again. One day, out of spite, the elderly woman turned on her sprinkler. Instead of watering her front lawn, it was set to water the sidewalk, preventing the children from even riding their bikes in front of her house.

Not being old enough to cross the street on their own, one of their favorite pastimes came to a standstill. Then a smile spread across one child's face, and as he whispered his idea to the others, smiles spread throughout the group. Each kid ran home with a mission. On that sunny, cloudless day the children returned with their bikes—and their raincoats. Their bike ride became a wet and wild adventure, as they rode through the sprinklers, laughing harder than they had with their original game.

When you are faced with difficult circumstances, the decision is yours. You can let a seed of bitterness rob you of joy, like it did the old woman. Or you can let circumstances stretch your creativity and lead you in a new direction. Who knows, you may find yourself somewhere you never expected, grateful for the new opportunity.

CLASS OF 2001

31

THINGS ARE NOT ALWAYS WHAT THEY SEEM.

The LORD does not look at the things man looks at.
Man looks at the outward appearance,
but the LORD looks at the heart.
1 Samuel 16:7 NIV

32

Donna and Gillian had planned their trip to Hawaii for more than a year. All the planning in the world, however, could not have prepared them for the unexpected death of one of their dearest friends right before they were to leave. In silence, they boarded the plane. They were going to miss the funeral, but the tickets couldn't be changed. They had to go now—or never.

After the first leg of their trip, the plane was delayed. When their early afternoon connection finally departed after midnight, Donna expressed her frustration and anger. "We could have stayed for the funeral and still caught this stupid plane!" she muttered. Though a week on the beach lifted their spirits, Donna and Gillian's bitterness over the late flight remained.

Then shortly after arriving at the airport for their return trip, they were startled by a woman's cry, "My baby's stopped breathing!" No one moved—except Donna. As a nurse, she knew exactly what to do. She gave the baby CPR and helped calm the mother until the ambulance arrived. It wasn't until they were on the plane that Gillian and Donna realized a startling fact. If they had made the earlier flight the week before, they would have picked up their rental car earlier and surrendered it earlier on the day they left. They would not have been there for the baby and his mother.

Even when circumstances seem meaningless or contrary, God has a plan. What a privilege to see your part in it.

33

BLESSED ARE
THOSE WHO SEE
THE HAND OF GOD
IN THE HAPHAZARD,
INEXPLICABLE, AND
SEEMINGLY SENSELESS
CIRCUMSTANCES
OF LIFE.

*I am with you and will watch
over you wherever you go.
Genesis 28:15 NIV*

Driving a car pool to the zoo was one thing. Waiting in the parking lot for two hours for the drive home was quite another. Carol tried to read but decided a leisurely drive might relieve some of the anxiety she had been feeling lately. As she pulled out of the parking lot, a crack of thunder heralded an afternoon thunderstorm.

Down the road, a man and two young children stood shivering in the sudden rain. He held his thumb out tentatively. Carol never picked up hitchhikers, but she couldn't ignore someone who obviously needed help.

"My car broke down in the zoo parking lot," the stranger explained. "Could you please get me to a phone? I need to call someone who's waiting for us at Sammy's Café." Having time to kill, Carol insisted on driving them to the nearby restaurant.

During the drive, the man talked about the many tragedies he had suffered in his life and how God had worked through them. When they reached their destination, the man commented, "God works miracles through painful situations. You are so special to Him. He's going to bless you!"

As Carol drove back to the zoo, she couldn't help wondering. *Why hadn't the man used a phone at the zoo rather than hitchhiking?* Perhaps, because she needed to hear God's voice in a personal way that day. That was blessing enough.

35

THERE CAN BE NO SUCH THING AS A NECESSARY EVIL. FOR IF A THING IS REALLY NECESSARY, IT CANNOT BE AN EVIL AND IF IT IS AN EVIL, IT IS NOT NECESSARY.

This is what the LORD says: "Stand at the crossroads and look; ask for the ancient paths, ask where the good way is, and walk in it, and you will find rest for your souls."
Jeremiah 6:16 NIV

In the seventeenth century, Edinburgh was bustling with both aristocracy and peasants, all living in very close quarters. The Scottish city was built on a hilltop with many enclosed stairways leading down to the city gates below. Each stairway, or "close," was shared by numerous families whose front doors opened onto it. Each close had a gate at the top and one at the bottom that were locked at night for protection. But the plague still found its way inside.

As word reached Edinburgh that the plague was spreading through the low-lying countryside, the city gates were locked to all outsiders. But soon there was a small outbreak inside the city, in Mary King's Close. To prevent further spread of the disease, the city fathers decided upon a simple, yet heartless plan.

The gates to Mary King's Close were locked with all 400 residents inside. They were given no food or water and their cries of suffering were ignored, until finally there was only silence. Mary King's Close is locked to this day, a memorial to those whose deaths served as an easy solution.

When faced with a difficult decision, take time to make sure your solution is the best one, not simply the most expedient.

MANY RECEIVE ADVICE; ONLY THE WISE PROFIT BY IT.

*Pride only breeds quarrels, but wisdom
is found in those who take advice.*
Proverbs 13:10 *NIV*

CLASS OF
2001

After arguing heatedly for several hours about which type of water main to purchase for their city, the town council of Pacific Vista was still deadlocked. One member suggested, "Let's appoint a committee to confer with the city engineer in Los Angeles about this matter. If we can profit by another city's experience and learn from their mistakes, I think we should do so."

At that point, an angry councilman—obviously full of civic pride but little discretion—pounded his fist on the table and replied, "Why should we have to learn from the mistakes Los Angeles has made? Gentlemen, I contend that Pacific Vista is a big enough town to make its own mistakes!"

Most of us are surrounded by good advice at any given time.

- The books in our libraries are full of it.
- Pastors proclaim it weekly.
- People with highly varied experiences and backgrounds abound with it.
- Schools give access to it; labs report it.
- Commentators and columnists gush with it.

But all the good advice in the world is worth very little if it is ignored. Be one of the wise—value and apply the advice you receive.

THE ONLY WAY TO HAVE A FRIEND IS TO BE ONE.

A man that hath friends
must shew himself friendly.
Proverbs 18:24

CLASS OF
2001

Mary Lennox "was not an affectionate child and had never cared much for anyone." And that was not so difficult to understand. Ignored by her parents and raised by servants, she had no concept of what life was like outside of India. Other children called her "Mistress Mary Quite Contrary," because she didn't like to share and always insisted on having her own way.

When Mary was nine years old, her parents died of cholera, and she was sent to live at her uncle's home in England. The move did nothing to improve her disposition. She expected anyone and everyone to jump when she snapped her fingers.

Gradually, however, Mary began to change. Realizing how lonely she was, she asked a robin in the garden to be her friend. She began treating her maid with more respect. Won over by the guilelessness of her maid's little brother, Dickon, and craving his approval, Mary found herself seeking his advice. She even revealed to him the location of her secret garden. Eventually, Mary convinced her crippled cousin, Colin, to grab hold of life with both hands. By the last page of *The Secret Garden*, Mary's transformation is complete. She is happy with herself and surrounded by friends.

To make a friend, you first must make a decision to be a friend.

41

A CHRISTIAN MUST KEEP THE FAITH, BUT NOT TO HIMSELF.

Go ye into all the world, and
preach the gospel to every creature.
Mark 16:15

A small dog was struck by a car and tossed onto the shoulder of the road. A doctor, who just happened to be driving by, noticed that the dog was still alive, stopped his car, picked it up, and took it home with him. When the doctor had an opportunity to examine the dog closely, he found that it had suffered only minor cuts and abrasions. So he cleaned its wounds and carried it to the garage, where he intended to provide a temporary bed.

However, the dog wriggled free from his arms, jumped to the ground, and scampered off. "What an ungrateful dog," the doctor said to himself. He was glad that the dog had recovered so quickly but a little miffed that it had shown so little appreciation for his expert care.

The doctor thought no more about the incident until the next evening, when he heard a scratching at his front door. He opened the door to find that the little dog had returned with another injured dog at its side!

Be encouraged! You may never see the difference you make in someone's life or the difference that person will make in the lives of others, but those with whom you share God's love will *never* be the same.

YOU MAY LAUGH OUT LOUD IN THE FUTURE AT SOMETHING YOU'RE EATING YOUR HEART OUT OVER TODAY.

Our light affliction, which is but for a moment, worketh for us a far more exceeding and eternal weight of glory.
2 Corinthians 4:17

44

Trevor knew he was supposed to sit quietly in church and pay attention. But the gurgling and rumbling in his stomach had captured his full attention. He tried holding his breath, closing his eyes, even humming quietly to himself. But suddenly, what he feared most seemed inevitable. Noticing the panicked look on his face, his mother whispered, "Trevor, what's the matter?"

Trevor quickly whispered back, "I think I'm gonna be sick!" His mother told him that the restroom was at the back of the church. With that, Trevor darted up from the pew. He returned so quickly, that his mother was a little worried. "Trevor, did you make it to the bathroom?"

Trevor replied with a smile, "I didn't have to mom. In the back of the church, they had a nice little box right by the door that says, 'For the Sick.'"[3]

What did you worry about when you were a kid? Monsters under your bed? Being the shortest kid in the class? The tallest? Never being able to master a two-wheeler? As we grow older, childhood fears seem almost ridiculously small. But as a child, they seemed monumental.

Let hindsight teach you something about the problems that may be overwhelming you today. A molehill right in front of you can loom larger than the mountain on the horizon, merely because of where you're standing.

45

THE MORE WE LEARN
ABOUT THE WONDERS
OF OUR UNIVERSE, THE
MORE CLEARLY WE ARE
GOING TO PERCEIVE
THE HAND OF GOD.

*By faith we understand that the universe was
formed at God's command, so that what is seen
was not made out of what is visible.*

Hebrews 11:3 NIV

Beth focused her camera on the field of wildflowers. From a distance, it looked like a uniform blanket of purple. Closer inspection revealed individual flowers, similar in composition, yet each bearing a unique combination of leaves and petals. She finished the roll of film and called it a day.

It wasn't until she enlarged the wildflower photos, though, that she noticed it. Within each of the tiny purple flowers, which themselves were no larger than the eraser of a pencil, there was a ring of white. The enlargements revealed that the ring itself was made of a tiny circle of perfectly formed white flowers, each no bigger than the size of a pencil point. Without magnification, the intricate beauty these common wildflowers contained would have gone unnoticed.

God weaves hidden beauty into places too small to be seen by the human eye . . . distant planets, blood cells, DNA strands. But why the extravagance? Why go to the extra work, even if you are the Creator of the universe?

During the Renaissance period, artists carefully finished the backs of statues fashioned for churches. They did this even though they knew only the eyes of God would ever enjoy them. In the same way, God must take delight in the act of creation, as well as its outcome. As God's most precious creation, He takes delight in every detail that makes you who you are.

47

THE TEST OF COURAGE COMES WHEN WE ARE IN THE MINORITY; THE TEST OF TOLERANCE WHEN WE ARE IN THE MAJORITY.

Be on your guard; stand firm in the faith; be men of courage; be strong. Do everything in love.
1 Corinthians 16:13-14 NIV

Raoul Wallenberg was a Swedish diplomat in the 1940s. Though the Holocaust of World War II threatened many lives, Wallenberg's wasn't one of them. His work for the Swedish government put him in a safe and privileged position. Yet Wallenberg worked to help save the lives of Hungarian Jews.

Having business connections in Hungary, Wallenberg set up an office issuing fake passports. But he didn't stop there. He set up safe housing, soup kitchens, and hospitals for those he was extending bogus passports to. On one occasion, he saw Jews being loaded onto a train destined for the death camps. He demanded that all of the prisoners with passports get off the train. Prisoner's waved any piece of paper they could find at him—eyeglass prescriptions, driver's licenses, even deportation papers. He honored them all as passports, saving three hundred lives. It is estimated that during the war, Wallenberg offered diplomatic protection to approximately two hundred thousand Hungarian Jews—just because he felt it was the right thing to do.[4]

God chooses unlikely heroes. Take David, facing Goliath with nothing but a handful of stones, or Moses, raised in the privileged safety of Pharaohs house, yet leading the Israelites, simply because God asked him to. Doing the right thing, even when it doesn't seem very dramatic or noteworthy, takes courage. Has God hidden a hero inside of you?

THE MIND GROWS BY WHAT IT FEEDS ON.

*The mind controlled by
the Spirit is life and peace.*
Romans 8:6 NIV

What does the list of books and authors below have in common?

- *Tarzan,* by Edgar Rice Burroughs.
- *Alice's Adventures in Wonderland,* by Lewis Carroll.
- *The Divine Comedy,* by Dante.
- *Grimm's Fairy Tales,* by the Brothers Grimm.
- *The Merchant of Venice,* by William Shakespeare.
- Works by Francis Bacon, Miguel de Cervantes, Socrates, John Calvin, Martin Luther, and Homer.
- The American Heritage Dictionary.
- Mother Goose.
- The Bible.

The answer is that at some time in history, each of these books and authors was banned. Those who chose to read their words, if they could even obtain a copy in the first place, did so at their own risk. Today things have changed, at least in the United States. Here, individuals decide for themselves what they will read, watch, listen to, stand up for, and stand against.

Yet that parental admonition still rings true: With greater freedom, comes greater responsibility. What weighs heaviest when you form an opinion or make a decision? Your gut reaction? The general consensus? The way you were raised? And how do you respond when someone's opinion differs from your own? Do you jump on your soapbox? Feel threatened? Or do you listen with love? Giving careful consideration to what you believe, and why, gives you the strength you need to stand in support of the crowd or alone against it.[5]

THE GREATER PART OF OUR HAPPINESS DEPENDS ON OUR DISPOSITION AND NOT OUR CIRCUMSTANCES.

*I know how to live on almost nothing
or with everything. I have learned the
secret of contentment in every situation.*
Philippians 4:12 TLB

Kara pressed her face against the window of her train compartment. Even though the sun had set long ago, she didn't want to miss a thing. It was her first trip to Egypt, and everything seemed so different from her home in California. That morning, an exodus of angry cockroaches had greeted her when she turned on the hotel shower. And one quick surge from her blowdryer was enough to blackout the power on the entire floor. Egypt didn't feel like another country. It felt like another world.

After miles of dimly lit desert, her eyes were drawn to a flicker of light. As the train approached, she saw it was a fire, surrounded by tents. A group of men were nearby, laughing animatedly. A young boy was reading a book by firelight, a camel enjoying the blaze by his side. Kara immediately felt sorry for the boy. *Probably a student like me,* she thought. Only here he was trying to do his homework by firelight and sleeping in a makeshift tent. But something about the boy's expression, made her reconsider. Who was she to argue with such a contented smile?

Circumstances change daily. If your happiness depends solely on what's going on around you, it cannot last. But if your joy comes from what is going on inside you, you can carry it with you wherever you go.

53

TO BELIEVE IN GOD IS TO KNOW THAT THE RULES WILL BE FAIR— AND THAT THERE WILL BE MANY SURPRISES!

"I am the Way—yes, and the Truth and the Life."
John 14:6 TLB

Trina and Heather carefully placed their beach chairs by the edge of the water—close enough to get their feet wet but not so close that a wave would splash salt water on their books. By the third day of their family vacation, the sisters had it down to an exact science. Or so they thought.

One moment, Heather was seated next to Trina, reading. The next, Trina looked over and Heather was gone. Rolled up in her beach chair, Heather was tumbling end over end toward the ocean as the rogue wave receded. After the salt water was coughed up, the mountain of sand dislodged from her suit, and the convulsive laughter calmed to a controlled giggle, Heather turned to Trina and said, "You didn't even get wet! No fair!"

Sometimes, life just doesn't look fair. One person sits relaxing on the beach while another faces a mini-tidal wave trauma. One person wins the lottery while another faces financial ruin. One person's medical test results come back negative, another's positive.

But God is always with you in the face of every surprise, both welcome and unwelcome. It is your heart, and not your circumstances, that will determine whether each "surprise" will draw you away from Him, or even closer to His side.

I HAVE NEVER BEEN HURT BY ANYTHING I DIDN'T SAY.

Don't talk so much. You keep putting your foot in your mouth. Be sensible and turn off the flow!
Proverbs 10:19 TLB

A young attorney, just out of law school and beginning his first day on the job, sat down in the comfort of his brand-new office with a great sigh of satisfaction. He had worked long and hard for the opportunity to savor such a moment. Then noticing a prospective client coming toward his door, he tried to look busy and energetic.

Opening his legal pad and uncapping his pen, he picked up the telephone, and cradling it under his chin, began to write furiously. "Look, Harry, about that amalgamation deal," he said to an empty phone line. "I think I better run down to the factory and handle it personally. Yes. No. I don't think three million dollars will swing it. We better have Smith from LA meet us there. Okay. Get back to me."

Hanging up the phone, he put down his pen, looked up at his visitor, stood, extended his hand, and said in his most polite but confident attorney's voice, "Good morning. How might I help you?" The prospective client replied, "Actually, I'm just here to hook up your phone."

There's an old saying that goes, "A shut mouth gathers no foot." Sometimes the best thing to do is just keep your mouth shut!

WE TOO OFTEN LOVE THINGS AND USE PEOPLE, WHEN WE SHOULD BE USING THINGS AND LOVING PEOPLE.

Be devoted to one another in brotherly love.
Honor one another above yourselves.
Romans 12:10 NIV

One day, a boy at summer camp received a box of cookies from his mother. He ate a few, then placed the box under his bed. The next day, he discovered the cookies were gone. Later, a counselor who had been told of the theft saw a boy sitting behind a tree eating the stolen cookies. He sought out the victim and said, "Bill, I know who stole your cookies. Will you help me teach him a lesson?" The boy replied, "Well, I guess—but aren't you going to punish him?"

The counselor said, "Not directly—that would only make him hate you. I have an idea. But first I want you to ask your mother to send some more cookies." The boy did as the counselor asked, and a few days later, another box of cookies arrived.

The counselor then said, "The boy who stole your cookies is by the lake. I suggest you go down there and share your cookies with him." The boy protested, "But he's the one who stole the first ones from me!" "I know," said the counselor. "Let's see what happens."

An hour later, the counselor saw the boys coming up the hill together. The thief was earnestly trying to get his new friend to accept his compass in payment for the stolen cookies, while the victim just as adamantly refused, saying a few old cookies didn't matter all that much!

Often the best way to "get back at someone" is to show them God's love. You can usually make a friend in the process.

WHEN YOU FLEE TEMPTATION, DON'T LEAVE A FORWARDING ADDRESS.

*Now flee from youthful lusts and
pursue righteousness . . . with those
who call on the Lord from a pure heart.*
2 Timothy 2:22 NAS

CLASS OF 2001

Velazquez Polk and Janet Kuzmaak both grew up in Portland, Oregon, but their lives could not have been more different. Polk was a tough street kid who joined a gang at age ten and was eventually arrested for selling drugs. Kuzmaak was an honor student from an upper-class neighborhood.

In 1980, Kuzmaak's sister was raped and murdered. Because authorities never solved the crime, she came to regard every criminal as her sister's killer.

Eventually, Kuzmaak became a nurse at a major medical center, and Polk, released from jail in 1990, was given a job as her surgical aide.

Kuzmaak was furious. She didn't believe in rehabilitation for criminals. But she noticed that when Polk's gang-member friends tried to entice him to rejoin their ranks, he refused. He told her that he wanted to flee his old life and join a program to become a nurse's aide. She remembered that her sister had once befriended a man on parole, so she lobbied the hospital to pay Polk's tuition while she continued to monitor him.

Today, Kuzmaak and Polk are great friends. She helped him gain entrance into a world he barely knew existed. And he helped her sweep away the bitterness that had once poisoned her heart.

Change and growth are always possible if you turn from evil and refuse to look back.

WHATEVER YOU DISLIKE IN ANOTHER PERSON, TAKE CARE TO CORRECT IN YOURSELF.

"Why do you look at the speck of sawdust in your brother's eye and pay no attention to the plank in your own eye?"
Matthew 7:3 NIV

In *A Closer Walk,* Catherine Marshall writes:

One morning last week, God gave me an assignment: for one day I was to go on a "fast" from criticism. I was not to criticize anybody about anything.

For the first half of the day, I simply felt a void, almost as if I had been wiped out as a person. This was especially true at lunch. I listened to the others and kept silent. In our talkative family, no one seemed to notice. Bemused, I noted that the federal government, the judicial system, and the institutional church could apparently get along fine without my penetrating observations. But still I didn't see what this fast on criticism was accomplishing—until mid-afternoon.

That afternoon, a specific, positive vision for this life was dropped into my mind with God's unmistakable hallmark on it—joy! Ideas began to flow in a way I had not experienced in years. Now it was apparent what the Lord wanted me to see. My critical nature had not corrected a single one of the multitudinous things I found fault with. What it had done was to stifle my own creativity.

Before you are tempted to criticize someone, examine your own life. While you may not commit the same act or have the same habit you're about to criticize, you probably have some behavior that *could* be criticized. Don't stifle your creativity with criticism!

63

DEFINITION OF STATUS: BUYING SOMETHING YOU DON'T NEED WITH MONEY YOU DON'T HAVE TO IMPRESS PEOPLE YOU DON'T LIKE.

"They do all their deeds to be noticed by men."
Matthew 23:5 NAS

Guy de Maupassant's *The Necklace* is the story of a young woman, Mathilde, who desires desperately to be accepted into high society. One day her husband, an ordinary man, is given an invitation to an elegant ball. Mathilde borrows a necklace from a wealthy friend to wear to the occasion and receives many compliments from the aristocracy present during the evening. Sadly, she discovers later that night that she has lost the necklace.

Mathilde's husband borrows 36,000 francs in an effort to replace the lost jewelry. He is forced to tap every resource available to him. Finally, a look-alike necklace is created, and Mathilde gives it to her friend, without telling her what had happened.

For ten years, the couple slaves to pay back the borrowed francs, each of them working two jobs. They are forced to sell their home and live in a slum. One day after the debt had finally been paid, Mathilde runs into her well-to-do friend and confesses that the necklace she returned was not the one she borrowed. To her consternation, she learns that the necklace loaned to her had been made from fake gemstones! The borrowed necklace had been worth less than 500 francs.

Trying to "keep up appearances" almost always leads to "falling flat on your face."

I LIKE THE DREAMS OF THE FUTURE BETTER THAN THE HISTORY OF THE PAST.

Remember ye not the former things,
neither consider the things of old.
Behold, I will do a new thing.
Isaiah 43:18-19

A man once took his three-year-old daughter to an amusement park. It was her first visit to such a place, and she was in awe at the sights and sounds, especially the whirl and whiz of the rides. She begged her dad to let her ride one particular ride, even though it was considered the "scariest" ride for kids her age.

As she whipped around the corners in her kiddy car, she suddenly wrinkled up her face and let loose with a terrified cry. Her father, who was riding in the car with her, struggled to get her attention. With a big smile, he shouted over the roar of the ride, "This is fun!" When the little girl saw that he was not afraid, she began to laugh. A new experience that was initially terrifying had suddenly become enjoyable. In fact, she insisted on riding the same ride a second and third time!

What a comfort it is to know that our Heavenly Father will not only ride the new rides in life with us, but that the future is never scary to Him. He has good things planned for us. When we look into the future from our perspective, we may become frightened. But when we look at the future from God's perspective, we are far more likely to shout, "Let's go! Isn't this going to be fun?"

THE WAY TO GET TO THE TOP IS TO GET OFF YOUR BOTTOM.

How long will you lie down, O sluggard?
When will you arise from your sleep?
Proverbs 6:9 NAS

One day, in the fall of 1894, Guglielmo retreated to his room on the third floor of his parent's home. He had just spent his entire summer vacation reading books and filling notebooks with squiggly diagrams. Now the time had come to work.

He rose early every morning. He worked all day and long into the night, to the point that his mother became alarmed. He had never been a robust person, but now he was appallingly thin. His face was drawn, and his eyes were often glazed over with fatigue.

Finally, the day came when he announced his instruments were ready. He invited the family to his room, and pushing a button, he succeeded in ringing a bell on the first floor! While his mother was amazed, his father was not. He saw no use in being able to send a signal so short a distance. So Guglielmo labored on. Little by little, he made changes in his invention so he could send a signal from one hill to the next, and then beyond the hill. Eventually, his invention was perfected, partly by inspiration, but mostly by perseverance.

Guglielmo Marconi eventually was hailed as the inventor of wireless telegraphy—the forerunner of the radio. He not only received a Nobel prize in physics for his efforts but also a seat in the Italian senate and many honorary degrees and titles.

You can accomplish anything you set your heart on by combining your vision with hard work.

YOU ARE ONLY WHAT YOU ARE WHEN NO ONE IS LOOKING.

Not with eyeservice, as menpleasers;
but as the servants of Christ,
doing the will of God from the heart.
Ephesians 6:6

Joe Smith was a loyal carpenter who worked almost two decades for a successful contractor. The contractor called him into his office one day and said, "Joe, I'm putting you in charge of the next house we build. I want you to order all the materials and oversee the job from the ground up."

Joe accepted the assignment with great enthusiasm. He studied the blueprints and checked every measurement and specification. Suddenly, he had a thought. *If I'm really in charge, why couldn't I cut a few corners, use less expensive materials, and put the extra money in my pocket? Who will know? Once the house is painted, it will look great.*

So Joe set about his scheme. He ordered second-grade lumber and inexpensive concrete, put in cheap wiring, and cut every corner he could. When the home was finished, the contractor came to see it.

"What a fine job you've done!" he said. "You've been such a faithful carpenter to me all these years that I've decided to show you my gratitude by giving you a gift—this house."

Build well today. You will have to live with the character and reputation you construct.

TAKE TIME TO DELIBERATE; BUT WHEN THE TIME FOR ACTION ARRIVES, STOP THINKING AND GO ON.

Rise up; this matter is in your hands.
We will support you, so take courage and do it.
Ezra 10:4 NIV

As long as he could remember, Jason had wanted to be a police officer. It wasn't just the fact that he loved playing cops and robbers. Jason wanted to do something that mattered with his life.

After graduation, Jason had the chance to apply for a spot at the police academy. But first, came the interview. When the veteran officer pulled up a chair in front of him, Jason realized his childhood dream could rest upon this very moment. As he confidently answered each question, he felt the officer's approval. Jason knew he was doing well.

"One last question," the officer said. "Suppose you're called to help at the site of an explosion. There are numerous casualties. Nearby, you notice a woman has gone into labor. At the same time, you see a car, whose driver is obviously intoxicated, weaving down the road toward an elementary school. Then, you hear a cry from someone drowning in a nearby river, while a fight erupts next to you that could result in both injury and property damage. What do you do?"

Jason thought a moment, then replied, "Try and hide my uniform and mingle with the crowd?"

Some situations in life take more than just a cool head. They take a miracle. But prayer without the courage to act upon what you hear is useless.

73

THERE ARE TIMES WHEN SILENCE IS GOLDEN, OTHER TIMES IT IS JUST PLAIN YELLOW.

To everything there is a season . . .
a time to keep silence, and a time to speak.
Ecclesiastes 3:1,7

CLASS OF
2001

According to an old fable, three men once decided to engage in the religious practice of absolute silence. They mutually agreed to keep a "day of quiet" from dawn until the stroke of midnight, at which time a full moon was expected to rise from the horizon. They sat cross-legged for hours, concentrating on the distant horizon, eager for darkness to envelop them.

One of them unwittingly noted, "It's difficult not to say anything at all."

The second one replied, "Quiet. You're speaking during the time of silence!"

The third man sighed and then boasted, "Now I'm the only one who hasn't spoken yet."

A rap singer has updated some of the advice given in the book of Ecclesiastes:

- There's a time to speak up and a time to shut up.
- There's a time to hunker down and a time to go downtown.
- There's a time to talk and a time to walk.
- There's a time to be mellow and a time not to be yellow.

Silence can be good but never if it's the result of raw fear or lack of moral fiber.

EVERY JOB IS A SELF-PORTRAIT OF THE PERSON WHO DOES IT. AUTOGRAPH YOUR WORK WITH EXCELLENCE.

Daniel was preferred above the presidents and princes, because an excellent spirit was in him.
Daniel 6:3

A band of minstrels from a faraway land traveled about singing and playing their music in hopes of making a living. But they had not been doing well. Times were hard, and the common people had little money to spend on concerts, even though their fee was small.

The group met one evening to discuss their plight. "I see no reason for opening tonight," one said. "It's snowing, and no one will come out on a night like this." Another said, "I agree. Last night we performed for just a handful. Even fewer will come tonight."

The leader of the troupe responded, "I know you are discouraged. I am too. But we have a responsibility to those who might come. We will go on, and we will do the best job we possibly can. It is not the fault of those who come that others do not. They should not be punished with less than our best."

Heartened by his words, the minstrels gave their best performance ever. After the show, the old man called his troupe to him again. In his hand was a note handed to him by one of the audience members just before the doors closed behind him. Slowly the man read, "Thank you for a beautiful performance." It was signed simply, "Your King."

Even if no one else notices the quality of your work, God does. Do your best. Do it for Him!

DON'T ASK GOD FOR WHAT YOU THINK IS GOOD; ASK HIM FOR WHAT HE THINKS IS GOOD FOR YOU.

"This, then, is how you should pray:
'Our Father in heaven, hallowed be
your name, your kingdom come,
your will be done on earth as it is in heaven.'"
Matthew 6:9-10 NIV

During a prayer meeting one night, an elderly woman pleaded, "It really doesn't matter what You do with us, Lord, just have Your way with our lives." Adelaide Pollard, a rather well-known itinerant Bible teacher, overheard her prayer. At the time, she was deeply discouraged because she had been unable to raise the money she needed to go to Africa for missionary service. She was moved by this woman's sincere request of God, and when she went home that evening, she meditated on Jeremiah 18:3-4: *Then I went down to the potter's house, and, behold, he wrought a work on the wheels, And the vessel that he made of clay was marred in the hand of the potter: so he made it again another vessel, as seemed good to the potter to make it.*

Before retiring, Adelaide took pen in hand and wrote in hymn form her own prayer:

> Have Thine own way, Lord! Have Thine own way!
> Thou art the potter, I am the clay.
> Mold me and make me after Thy will,
> While I am waiting, yielded and still.

The best way to discover the purpose for your life is to give yourself, along with all your plans and dreams, to God. Then He can reveal and fulfill His plan for you. You won't be disappointed.

WITHOUT GOD, THE WORLD WOULD BE A MAZE WITHOUT A CLUE.

This God is our God for ever and ever;
he will be our guide even to the end.
Psalm 48:14 NIV

CLASS OF
2001

Up in the choir loft of the old church on Main Street, there was an organ. In between holiday celebrations, it sat idle collecting dust—and mice. The mice that were born inside the organ considered their home a kind of quiet maze, filled with hammers, wires, and chimes—until Christmas Eve.

As the first notes from the slightly-off-tune instrument filled the home of the mice with music, they were awe-struck. How their home moved and roared! What talent and timbre it possessed! But one small mouse wondered if there was more to the mystery. As he strained to pull himself through a small opening near the floorboards, he saw a woman carefully placing her fingers on the yellowed keys. The mouse realized it was the woman, not the organ itself, who possessed this wonderful gift of music. He ran back to tell everyone there was someone greater than the organ itself—someone who was making it sing!

The other mice laughed and laughed. Who could believe such a preposterous tale? After all, hadn't they seen the hammers move by themselves with their own eyes?

There's more to life, and truth, than meets the eye. So when someone tells you "seeing is believing," remember, *Faith is being sure of what we hope for and certain of what we do not see* (Hebrews 11:1 NIV).

OPPORTUNITIES ARE SELDOM LABELED.

Seek, and ye shall find; knock,
and it shall be opened unto you.
Matthew 7:7

In 1970, Wally started baking chocolate chip cookies for his friends, using a recipe and procedure that had been passed down from his Aunt Della. For five years he gave away every batch he made, even though people often told him his cookies were so good he should go into business. Wally had other ideas though. He was determined to become a big-time show business manager.

Then one day a friend, B. J. Gilmore, told him that she had a friend who could put up the money for a cookie-making business. Her friend never made the investment, but Wally got some of his own friends—including Jeff Wall, Helen Reddy, and Marvin Gaye—to invest some money. Then he was off and running.

Originally, he intended to open only one store on Sunset Boulevard, just enough to "make a living." After all, his was the only store in the world dedicated to the sale of nothing but chocolate chip cookies. But business grew virtually overnight. Wally's "Famous Amos Chocolate Chip Cookies" were soon distributed worldwide. Wally himself became a spokesman for other products, from eggs to airlines, to a telephone company. While he once dreamed of managing stars, he is now one in his own right!

Sometimes dreams come through the back door. Keep it unlocked!

DON'T BE DISCOURAGED; EVERYONE WHO GOT WHERE HE IS, STARTED WHERE HE WAS.

Though your beginning was insignificant,
Yet your end will increase greatly.
Job 8:7 NAS

During the late 1960s, a couple was vacationing in the California mountains when they noticed a pleasant-looking young man sitting by a bridge near their hotel. Day after day they saw him sitting in the same spot. At first, they assumed he was fishing, but after a few days they realized he was doing nothing—just sitting and staring into space. Finally, on the last day of their vacation, they decided to approach the young man. "Why do you sit in that one spot all day, every day?" they asked.

He replied with a smile, "I happen to believe in reincarnation. I believe that I have lived many times before and that I will have many lives following this one. So this life I'm sitting out."

In reality, it's impossible for any of us to "sit out" life. Each day, we are either moving forward or backward, getting stronger or weaker, moving higher or lower. Each of us begins every new day with a fresh opportunity to change tomorrow's starting point.

You only have one chance at life. What will you do today to make your tomorrow better?

MATURITY DOESN'T COME WITH AGE; IT COMES WITH ACCEPTANCE OF RESPONSIBILITY.

When I was a child, I spake as a child, I understood as a child, I thought as a child: but when I became a man, I put away childish things.
1 Corinthians 13:11

CLASS OF
2001

A number of definitions of maturity have been offered by experts, but these are perhaps among the best-understood by the average person:

- Maturity is when you want to have a puppy to call your own, AND you remember on your own to give it food and water every day.
- Maturity is when you know how to dress yourself, AND you remember to put your dirty clothes in the laundry hamper after you've taken them off.
- Maturity is when you are capable of using a telephone, AND you know how to keep your calls short so others can have access to the phone.
- Maturity is when you are old enough to stay at home alone, AND you can be trusted to have friends over.
- Maturity is when you are old enough to drive the car, AND you are responsible enough to pay for the gasoline you use.
- Maturity is when you are old enough to stay up late, AND you are wise enough to go to bed early.

If you want to know how mature you really are, measure your ability to take responsibility for your personal choices.

THE CAPACITY TO CARE GIVES LIFE ITS DEEPEST SIGNIFICANCE.

*Carry each other's burdens, and in this
way you will fulfill the law of Christ.*
Galatians 6:2 NIV

When Ryan found out his dog, Mulder, was going to have puppies, every morning was a race to the laundry room to see if the miracle had occurred while he slept. One morning, Ryan was rewarded by the sight of nine squirming balls of fur. Knowing that his parents had said he could keep only one, Ryan made the difficult choice of deciding which one would stay and which ones would be given away.

Six weeks later, Ryan made a cardboard sign that he carefully attached to the mailbox in front of his house. It read, "Cute puppies. FREE!" After several weeks, only two of the puppies had been given away. So Ryan decided to try a new approach. His new sign read, "Five cute puppies and only one really ugly one. Free to a good home!" The puppies were gone within the day. Every person who knocked on the door wanted to come to the rescue of that one poor, ugly pup.

Plenty of people want to help the underdog. Too often they're just not sure of how to go about it. Who has God put in your life that could use your help today? It could be a gift of time, finances, elbow grease, or maybe just friendship. But reaching out to help someone doesn't deplete your resources. It actually enlarges your capacity to care.

THE EASIEST WAY TO DIGNITY IS HUMILITY.

God sets himself against the proud,
but he shows favor to the humble.
James 4:6 NLT

CLASS OF
2001

A group of businessmen went to a remote mountain retreat for a weekend of leadership training. Expecting graphs, statistics, and pep talks, they were more than a little wary when they were asked to trade their notebooks in for shovels. Next, their boss, Mr. Clarkson, gave them their assignment for the weekend. "I want you to dig a ditch two feet wide and ten inches deep around the perimeter of the cabin." With those words, Mr. Clarkson walked back to the cabin and disappeared inside.

At first the group was silent, stunned by the ridiculous task that lay ahead. But soon the silence turned into questioning the purpose of the exercise, arguing if nine inches was close enough to ten, and complaining about having risen to the top of the corporate ladder only to be forced to do manual labor. Finally, Bill, a newcomer to the group, turned to the others and said, "Who cares why we have to do this. Let's just do it and get it over with!"

With those words, the cabin door opened and Mr. Clarkson reappeared. "Gentlemen," he said as he grabbed Bill's hand, "I'd like you to meet your new vice-president."

The "whys" of what you have to do in life won't always be clear. But as long as you understand the "hows," the best thing to do is get to work.

THE HAPPIEST PEOPLE DON'T NECESSARILY HAVE THE BEST OF EVERYTHING. THEY JUST MAKE THE BEST OF EVERYTHING.

I have learned, in whatsoever state I am,
therewith to be content. I can do all things
through Christ which strengtheneth me.
Philippians 4:11,13

A story is told of identical twins: one a hope-filled optimist who often said, "Everything is coming up roses," and the other, a sad and hopeless pessimist who continually expected the worst to happen. The concerned parents of the twins brought them to a psychologist in the hope that he might be able to help them balance the boys' personalities.

The psychologist suggested that on the twins' next birthday, the parents put them in separate rooms to open their gifts. "Give the pessimist the best toys you can afford," the psychologist said, "and give the optimist a box of manure." The parents did as he had suggested.

When they peeked in on the pessimistic twin, they heard him complaining, "I don't like the color of this toy. I'll bet this toy will break! I don't like to play this game. I know someone who has a bigger toy than this!"

Tiptoeing across the corridor, the parents peeked in and saw their optimistic son gleefully throwing manure up in the air. He was giggling as he said, "You can't fool me! Where there's this much manure, there's gotta be a pony!"

How are you looking at life today? As an accident waiting to happen, or a blessing about to be received?

LEARN BY EXPERIENCE—PREFERABLY OTHER PEOPLE'S.

*All these things happened to them
as examples—as object lessons to us—
to warn us against doing the same things.*
1 Corinthians 10:11 TLB

94

Famous World War II general, George S. Patton Jr., was an avid reader and student of history. He wrote to his son in 1944: "To be a successful soldier, you must know history. Read it objectively. In Sicily, I decided, as a result of my information, observations, and instincts, that the enemy was not capable of initiating another large-scale attack. I bet my shirt on it and I was right."

When he observed the situation in Normandy on July 2, 1944, Patton immediately wrote Eisenhower that the German Schlieffen Plan of 1914 could be applied. A month later, the operation brought about the German defeat in Normandy.

Patton's uncanny ability to predict the enemy's actions most likely was developed by thousands of hours of reading history. Historical parallels were constantly on his mind.

The book that perhaps influenced Patton most was Ardant du Picque's *Battle Studies*. Patton used it to help solve the problem of getting infantry to advance through enemy artillery fire.

If you are interested in being a success in life, immerse yourself in history, especially the life stories of successful people. Read it objectively. You will learn from the mistakes and failures of others, as well as their successes and triumphs.

CLASS OF 2001

95

IT'S NOT HARD TO MAKE DECISIONS WHEN YOU KNOW WHAT YOUR VALUES ARE.

Daniel purposed in his heart that
he would not defile himself.
Daniel 1:8

Marshall Field once offered the following twelve principles for obtaining a sound sense of values:

1. Understanding the value of time.

2. Appreciating the power of perseverance.

3. Basking in the pleasure of working.

4. Appreciating the worth of simplicity.

5. Valuing good character.

6. Utilizing the power of kindness.

7. Appreciating the influence of example.

8. Honoring the obligation of duty.

9. Utilizing the wisdom of economy.

10. Nurturing the virtue of patience.

11. Encouraging the development of talent.

12. Appreciating the joy of originating.

Can you state the core principles of your value system today? Solid values are like unblemished, evenly-hewn stones. When you build your life with them, you can be sure they will serve as a strong foundation for making good decisions and appropriate choices.

I AM ONLY ONE; BUT STILL I AM ONE. I CANNOT DO EVERY-THING, BUT STILL I CAN DO SOMETHING; I WILL NOT REFUSE TO DO THE SOMETHING I CAN DO.

*Under his (Christ's) direction the whole body
is fitted together perfectly, and each part
in its own special way helps the other parts.*
Ephesians 4:16 TLB

Jewish physician, Boris Kornfeld, was imprisoned in Siberia. There he worked in surgery, helping both the staff and prisoners. He met a Christian whose name is unknown but whose quiet faith and frequent reciting of the Lord's Prayer had an impact on Dr. Kornfeld.

One day while repairing the slashed artery of a guard, Dr. Kornfeld seriously considered suturing the artery in such a way that the guard would slowly die of internal bleeding. The violence he recognized in his own heart appalled him, and he found himself saying, "Forgive us our sins as we forgive those who sin against us." Afterward, he began to refuse to obey various inhumane, immoral, prison-camp rules, even though he knew his quiet rebellion would place his life in danger.

One afternoon, he examined a patient who had undergone an operation to remove cancer. He saw in the man's eyes a depth of spiritual misery that moved him with compassion, and he told him his entire story, including a confession of his secret faith. That very night, Dr. Kornfeld was murdered as he slept. But his testimony was not in vain. The patient who heard his confession had become a Christian as a result. He survived the prison camp and went on to tell the world about life in the gulag.

That patient was Aleksandr Solzhenitsyn, who became one of the leading Russian writers of the twentieth century. He revealed to the world the horrors of the prison camps and perils of Russian communism.

You can make a difference. You can change your world. God has a wonderful plan for your life.

CLASS OF 2001

POLITENESS GOES FAR, YET COSTS NOTHING.

A kind man benefits himself.
Proverbs 11:17 NIV

In 1865, after General Ulysses S. Grant had moved his occupying army into Shiloh, he ordered a 7:00 P.M. curfew for the city. One distinguished Southern lady, Mrs. Johnson, was seen walking near the army's downtown headquarters near the curfew time.

General Grant approached her and said, "Mrs. Johnson, it's too dangerous for you to be out here. I'm going to ask two of my officers to escort you home." Surprisingly, the woman replied determinedly, "I won't go."

Grant smiled, went back into his headquarters, and returned in a few minutes wearing an overcoat that covered his insignia and rank.

"May I walk with you, Mrs. Johnson?" he asked.

"Why, yes," Mrs. Johnson replied, nearly blushing. "I'm always glad to have a gentleman as an escort."

Grant understood that this Southern woman could not bring herself to walk with a Union soldier, but she could allow herself to be escorted by a man she saw as a gentleman. Good manners and genuine politeness go a long way toward covering many of our faults, mistakes, and differences.

WE SHOULD BEHAVE TO OUR FRIENDS AS WE WOULD WISH OUR FRIENDS TO BEHAVE TO US.

*As ye would that men should do
to you, do ye also to them likewise.*
Luke 6:31

President Harry Truman had a reputation for honesty and loyalty. He stood by his friends even when it meant the risk of public ridicule.

Jim Pendergast was a friend from Truman's army days. Jim and his dad urged Truman to run for office—a judgeship in rural Jackson county. A year later, Truman did so, and with Pendergast's support, he won the election. As judge, he didn't always agree with Pendergast's practices. Tom once said to a group of contractors who had asked him to influence Truman, "I told you he was the hardheadedest, orneriest man in the world; there isn't anything I can do."

Unfortunately, Pendergast's penchant for horse racing caused him to be investigated for income tax evasion. He confessed, was fined, and sentenced to serve fifteen months in a federal penitentiary. When Pendergast died during Truman's vice-presidency, Truman didn't hesitate to fly to Kansas City for the funeral. "He was always my friend," Truman said of him, "and I have always been his."

True friendship is not based on what a friend does for you but on what he means to you.

CHARACTER IS WHAT YOU ARE IN THE DARK.

The integrity of the upright shall guide them.
Proverbs 11:3

Have you ever watched an icicle form one drop at a time? If the water is clean, the icicle remains clear and sparkles brightly in the sun; but if the water is slightly muddy, the icicle looks cloudy, its beauty spoiled.

Character is formed in the same way. Each thought and feeling, every decision—about matters both great and small—adds a layer. Every outside influence that touches our minds and souls—impressions, experiences, visual images, the words of others—helps define our character.

We must remain concerned at all times about the "droplets" that we allow to drip into our lives. Just as habits born of hate, falsehood, and evil intent mar and eventually destroy us, acts that develop habits of love, truth, and goodness silently mold and fashion us into the image of God.

When you build a clear, sparkling character, the light reflected through you will pierce the darkness around you.

ADVERSITY CAUSES SOME MEN TO BREAK, OTHERS TO BREAK RECORDS.

If thou faint in the day of adversity,
thy strength is small.
Proverbs 24:10

As a senior in high school, Jim averaged a batting average of .427 and led his team in home runs. He also quarterbacked his football team, which made it to the state semifinals. Jim later became a pitcher for the New York Yankees.

That's a remarkable achievement for any athlete. But it's an almost unbelievable one for Jim, who was born without a right hand.

A little boy who had only parts of two fingers on one of his hands once came to Jim in the clubhouse after a Yankees game and said, "They call me 'Crab' at camp. Did kids ever tease you?"

"Yea," Jim replied. "Kids used to tell me that my hand looked like a foot." And then he asked the boy an all-important question, "Is there anything you can't do?" The boy answered, "No."

"Well, I don't think so either," Jim responded.

A limitation can only hold us back if we *think* it can. God certainly doesn't see us as limited, for He has given us unlimited potential. When we begin to see ourselves the way God sees us, there are no records we can't break!

107

LEARN TO SAY "NO"; IT WILL BE OF MORE USE TO YOU THAN TO BE ABLE TO READ LATIN.

Just say a simple yes or no,
so that you will not sin.
James 5:12 TLB

The former president of Baylor University, Rufus C. Burleson, once told an audience,

How often I have heard my father paint in glowing words the honesty of his old friend Colonel Ben Sherrod. When he was threatened with bankruptcy and destitution in old age and staggering under a debt of $850,000, a contemptible lawyer told him, "Colonel Sherrod, you are hopelessly ruined, but if you will furnish me $5,000 as a witness fee, I can pick a technical flaw in the whole thing and get you out of it."

The grand old Alabaman said, "Your proposition is insulting. I signed the notes in good faith, and the last dollar shall be paid even if charity digs my grave and buys my shroud." He carried me and my brother Richard once especially to see that incorruptible old man, and his face and words are imprinted upon my heart and brain.

People will remember us for the promises we keep and the honest words we speak, especially when we could have profited by not telling the truth. Your word is your greatest asset, and honesty is your best virtue.

MEN ARE ALIKE IN THEIR PROMISES. IT IS ONLY IN THEIR DEEDS THAT THEY DIFFER.

Many a man claims to have unfailing love,
but a faithful man who can find?
Proverbs 20:6 NIV

When Teddy Roosevelt was asked to give a speech to the Naval War College in Newport, Rhode Island, on June 2, 1897, his theme was "Readiness." He insisted the only way to keep peace was to be ready for war, and the only way to be ready for war was to enlarge the navy. It was a rousing, patriotic speech.

The following February, the *Maine* was blown up, killing two hundred and sixty four sailors, and Americans across the land cried, "Remember the *Maine!*" In April, President McKinley asked Congress to declare war.

For obvious reasons, Americans were not surprised that Roosevelt backed the war effort. Most Americans *were* surprised, however, when Teddy Roosevelt resigned from his position as assistant secretary of the navy three weeks after the war declaration so that he'd be ready to fight. His friends told him he was crazy for throwing away his political future. His wife was against it. Yet all who knew Roosevelt well knew their protests were in vain. He had to join the effort.

Roosevelt later wrote that he wanted to be able to tell his children why he had fought in the war, not why he *hadn't* fought in it. As far as he was concerned, a person simply couldn't preach one thing and then do another. It is this approach to life that will separate you from the pack and cause you to become a great man or woman.

CLASS OF 2001

111

DON'T CROSS YOUR
BRIDGES UNTIL YOU
GET TO THEM. WE
SPEND OUR LIVES
DEFEATING OURSELVES
CROSSING BRIDGES
WE NEVER GET TO.

*"Don't be anxious about tomorrow.
God will take care of your tomorrow too.
Live one day at a time."*
Matthew 6:34 TLB

During the four-week siege of Tientsin, during the Boxer Rebellion of June 1900, Herbert Hoover helped erect barricades around the foreign compound and organized all the able-bodied men into a protective force to man them. Mrs. Hoover went to work too, helping set up a hospital, taking her turn nursing the wounded, rationing food, and serving tea every afternoon to those on sentry duty. Like her husband, she remained calm and efficient throughout the crisis, and even seemed to enjoy the excitement.

One afternoon, while sitting at home playing solitaire to relax after her work at the hospital, a shell suddenly burst nearby. She ran to the back door and discovered a big hole in the backyard. A little later, a second shell hit the road in front of the house. Then came a third shell. This one burst through one of the windows of the house and demolished a post by the staircase.

Several reporters covering the siege rushed into the living room to ensure that she was all right. They found her calmly seated at the card table. "I don't seem to be winning this hand," she remarked coolly, "but that was the third shell and therefore, the last one for the present anyway. Their pattern is three in a row." Then she suggested brightly, "Let's go and have tea."

If you think about it, you will realize most of the things you worry about never happen. Instead of worrying, relax and use your mental energy for more important things.

113

YOU MUST HAVE LONG-RANGE GOALS TO KEEP YOU FROM BEING FRUSTRATED BY SHORT-RANGE FAILURES.

Let us fix our eyes on Jesus, the author and perfecter of our faith, who for the joy set before him endured the cross, scorning its shame, and sat down at the right hand of the throne of God.

Hebrews 12:2 NIV

114

In 1877, George Eastman dreamed that the wonderful world of photography might be accessible to the average person. At the time, photographers working outdoors had to carry multiple pieces of bulky equipment and a corrosive agent called silver nitrate. Eastman theorized that if he could eliminate most of this equipment, he would have something.

Working in a bank by day, he spent his nights reading books on chemistry and magazines about photography. He took foreign language lessons, so he could read information published in France and Germany. Then with a partner, he began his own company in 1881. Almost immediately, a problem arose with the new "dry plates" he had invented. Eastman refunded the money to those who had purchased them and returned to his lab. Three months and four hundred seventy two experiments later, he came up with the durable emulsion for which he had searched!

Eastman spent many nights sleeping in a hammock at his factory after long days designing equipment. To replace the glass used for photographic plates, he created a roll of thin, flexible material now known as film. To replace heavy tripods, he developed a pocket camera. By 1895, photography was at last available to the "common man."

George Eastman's long-term vision kept him motivated even when four hundred seventy one experiments failed. Keeping your ultimate dream in mind, set short, attainable goals, and before you even know it, your vision will be a reality!

CLEAR YOUR MIND OF CAN'T.

I can do all things through
Christ which strengtheneth me.
Philippians 4:13

Harry Houdini, who won fame as an escape artist early in the twentieth century, issued a challenge wherever he went. He claimed he could be locked in any jail cell in the country and set himself free within minutes. Indeed, he made good on this claim in every city he visited.

One time, however, something seemed to go wrong. Houdini entered a jail cell in his street clothes. The heavy metal doors clanged shut behind him, and he took from his belt a concealed piece of strong, but flexible metal. He set to work on the lock to his cell, but soon realized something was wrong. He worked for thirty minutes without success. An hour passed. This was much longer than it usually took to free himself. Houdini began to sweat and pant in exasperation. Still, he could not pick the lock.

Finally, after laboring for two hours, frustrated and barely fending off a sense of failure, Houdini leaned against the door. To his amazement, it swung open! It had never been locked in the first place!

How many times are challenges impossible simply because we think they are? When we focus our minds and energy on them and strike the word "can't" from our vocabulary, impossible tasks are almost always transformed into attainable goals.

THE FUTURE BELONGS TO THOSE WHO BELIEVE IN THE BEAUTY OF THEIR DREAMS.

"Anything is possible if you have faith."
Mark 9:23 TLB

Grace Hopper was born with a desire to discover how things worked. At age seven, her curiosity led her to dismantle every clock in her childhood home! When she grew up, she eventually completed a doctorate in mathematics at Yale University. During World War II, Grace joined the navy and was assigned to the navy's computation project at Harvard University. There she met "Harvard Mark I," the first fully-functional, digital computing machine.

Unlike the clocks in her childhood home, "Harvard Mark I" had seven-hundred fifty thousand parts and five-hundred miles of wire! While most experts believed computers were too complicated and expensive for anyone but highly trained scientists to use, Grace thought otherwise. Her goal was to understand how computers work and then to simplify the intimidating processes so more people could use them. Her work gave rise to the programming language COBOL.

As late as 1963, each large computer had its own unique master language. Grace became an advocate for a universally-accepted language. She had the audacity to envision a day when computers would be small enough to sit on a desk, more powerful than "Harvard Mark I," and useful in offices, schools, and homes. At the age of seventy-nine, she retired from the U.S. Navy with a rank of rear admiral. But more important to her, she had lived to see her dream of personal computers come true!

Believe in your dreams. With God, all things are possible.

CLASS OF 2001

119

THE FUTURE BELONGS TO THOSE WHO SEE POSSIBILITIES BEFORE THEY BECOME OBVIOUS.

The vision is yet for an appointed time . . .
it will surely come, it will not tarry.
Habakkuk 2:3

CLASS OF 2001

ENIAC was one of the first computers to use electronic circuits, which made for lightning-fast calculations. At first, Thomas J. Watson Jr., the former chairman of IBM, saw no use for it. He said, "I reacted to ENIAC the way some people probably reacted to the Wright brothers' airplane. It didn't move me at all. I couldn't see this gigantic, costly, unreliable device as a piece of business equipment."

A few weeks later, he and his father wandered into a research office at IBM and saw an engineer with a high-speed punch-card machine hooked up to a black box. When asked what he was doing, the engineer replied, "Multiplying with radio tubes." The machine was tabulating a payroll at one-tenth the time it took the standard punch-card machine to do so. Watson was impressed. He and his dad liked the idea of having the world's first commercial electronic calculator.

That's how IBM entered the world of electronics. Within a year, they had electronic circuits that both multiplied and divided, and at that point, electronic calculators became truly useful. Thousands of IBM 604s were sold.

What wasn't yet obvious to Thomas Watson was obvious to the engineer working in the research department. Always keep your eyes and ears open; you never know what you might discover. Look for the possibilities around you.

121

WHEN I WAS A YOUNG
MAN I OBSERVED
THAT NINE OUT OF
TEN THINGS I DID
WERE FAILURES. I
DIDN'T WANT TO BE A
FAILURE, SO I DID TEN
TIMES MORE WORK.

He becometh poor that dealeth with a slack hand:
but the hand of the diligent maketh rich.
Proverbs 10:4

122

Early in the 1989 basketball season, Michigan faced Wisconsin. With just seconds left in the fourth quarter, Michigan's Rumeal Robinson found himself at the foul line. His team was trailing by one point, and he knew that if he could sink both shots, Michigan would win. Sadly, Rumeal missed both shots. Wisconsin upset the favored Michigan, and Rumeal went to the locker room feeling devastated and embarrassed.

His dejection, however, spurred him into action and ignited his determination. He decided that at the end of each practice for the rest of the season, he was going to shoot one hundred extra foul shots. Shoot 'em he did!

The moment came when Rumeal stepped to the foul line in yet another game, again with the opportunity to make two shots. This time, there were only three seconds left in overtime, and the game was the NCAA finals! *Swish* went the first shot! And *swish* went the second. Those two points gave Michigan the victory and the collegiate national championship for the season.

Have you just failed at something? Don't give up. Instead, work harder. Success is possible!

LUCK IS A MATTER OF PREPARATION MEETING OPPORTUNITY.

Make the most of every opportunity.
Colossians 4:5 NIV

We can learn a great deal from the Alaskan Bull Moose. Each fall during the breeding season, the males of the species battle for dominance. They literally go head-to-head, antlers crunching together as they collide. When the antlers are broken, defeat is ensured, since a moose's antlers are its only weapon.

Generally speaking, the heftiest moose with the largest and strongest antlers wins. Therefore, the battle is nearly always predetermined the summer before. It is then that the moose eat nearly 'round the clock. The one that consumes the best diet for growing antlers and gaining weight will be the victor. Those who eat inadequately will have weaker antlers and less bulk. The fight itself involves far more brawn than brain and more reliance on bulk than on skill.

Many people stand around waiting for their "big break"— some extraordinary opportunity that will catapult them to success. And yet, successful people are almost always those who take the time and effort to prepare to seize opportunities when they present themselves. You won't find them sitting around waiting for a "break." You will find them studying, practicing, researching, developing, and honing their skills and talents. Take a lesson from the Alaskan Bull Moose—prepare today for tomorrow's opportunities.

CLASS OF 2001

125

THE MOST VALUABLE OF ALL TALENTS IS THAT OF NEVER USING TWO WORDS WHEN ONE WILL DO.

In the multitude of words there wanteth not sin:
but he that refraineth his lips is wise.
Proverbs 10:19

Albert Einstein is reputed to have had a wholesome disregard for the tyranny of custom. One evening, the president of Swarthmore College hosted a dinner held in Einstein's honor. He was not scheduled to speak, but after the award was made, the audience clamored "Speech, speech," and the president turned the podium over to him.

Einstein reluctantly came forward and said only this: "Ladies and gentlemen, I am very sorry but I have nothing to say." And then he sat down. A few seconds later, he stood up again and said, "In case I do have something to say, I'll come back."

Some six months later, Einstein wired the president of the college with this message: "Now I have something to say." Another dinner was scheduled, and this time, Einstein made a speech.

If you have nothing to say, it's wise to say nothing. If you do have something to say, it's wise to say it in as few words as possible. As the old saying goes, "If your mind should go blank, don't forget to turn off the sound."

LAZINESS IS OFTEN MISTAKEN FOR PATIENCE.

Let us lay aside every weight, and the sin which doth so easily beset us, and let us run with patience the race that is set before us.
Hebrews 12:1

128

Henry Ward Beecher, one of the most powerful preachers in American history, gave this illustration in one of his sermons:

"The lobster, when left high and dry among the rocks, has no sense and energy enough to work his way back to the sea, but waits for the sea to come to him. If it does not come, he remains where he is, and dies, although the slightest exertion would enable him to reach the waves, which are perhaps tossing and tumbling within a yard of him.

"There is a tide in human affairs that casts men into 'tight places,' and leaves them there, like stranded lobsters. If they choose to lie where the breakers have flung them, expecting some grand billow to take them on its big shoulders and carry them to smooth water, the chances are that their hopes will never be realized."

Laziness is doing nothing, hoping nothing, being nothing. Patience on the other hand, means working on in hope that what you're waiting for will eventually come to pass, but you will continue to work on even if it doesn't.

ONE-HALF THE TROUBLE OF THIS LIFE CAN BE TRACED TO SAYING "YES" TOO QUICKLY AND NOT SAYING "NO" SOON ENOUGH.

Seest thou a man that is hasty in his words?
there is more hope of a fool than of him.
Proverbs 29:20

A man who had been quite successful in the manufacturing business decided to retire. He called in his son to tell him of his decision, saying, "Son, it's all yours as of the first of next month." The son, while eager to take over the firm and exert his own brand of leadership, also realized what a big responsibility he was facing. "I'd be grateful for any words of advice you have to give me," he said to his father.

The father advised, "Well, I've made a success of this business because of two principles: reliability and wisdom. First, take reliability. If you promise goods by the tenth of the month, no matter what happens, you must deliver by the tenth. Your customers won't understand any delay. They'll see a delay as failure. So even if it costs you overtime, double time, or golden time, you must deliver on your promise."

The son mulled this over for a few moments and then asked, "And wisdom?" The father shot back: "Wisdom is never making such a stupid promise in the first place."

Carefully weigh your ability to back up your words with evidence, and be sure you can deliver on a promise before you make it. A large part of your reputation is your ability to keep your word.

CLASS OF 2001

131

I WOULD RATHER FAIL IN THE CAUSE THAT SOMEDAY WILL TRIUMPH THAN TRIUMPH IN A CAUSE THAT SOMEDAY WILL FAIL.

Now thanks be unto God, which always causeth us to triumph in Christ.
2 Corinthians 2:14

When Honorious was emperor of Rome, the great coliseum was often filled to overflowing with spectators who came from near and far to watch the state-sponsored games. Part of the sport consisted of human beings doing battle with wild beasts or one another—to the death. The assembled multitudes made a holiday of such sport and found the greatest delight when a human being died.

One such day, a Syrian monk named Telemachus was part of the vast crowd in the arena. Telemachus was cut to the core by the utter disregard he saw for the value of human life. He leaped from the spectator stands into the arena during a gladiatorial show and cried out, "This thing is not right! This thing must stop!"

Because he had interfered, the authorities commanded that Telemachus be run through with a sword, which was done. He died but not in vain. His cry kindled a small flame in the nearly burned-out conscience of the people, and within a matter of months, the gladiatorial combats came to an end.

The greater the wrong, the louder we must cry out against it. The finer the cause, the louder we must applaud.

133

CARVE YOUR NAME ON HEARTS AND NOT ON MARBLE.

The only letter I need is you yourselves! . . .
They can see that you are a letter from Christ,
written by us. . . . not one carved
on stone, but in human hearts.
2 Corinthians 3:2-3 TLB

When Salvation Army officer Shaw saw the three men before him, tears sprang into his eyes. Shaw was a medical missionary who had just arrived in India. He had been assigned to a leper colony the Salvation Army was taking over. The three men before him had manacles and fetters binding their hands and feet. Their bonds were painfully cutting into their diseased flesh. Captain Shaw turned to the guard and said, "Please unfasten the chains."

"It isn't safe," the guard protested. "These men are dangerous criminals as well as lepers!"

"I'll be responsible," Captain Shaw said. "They are suffering enough." He then reached out, took the keys, knelt, tenderly removed the shackles from the men, and treated their bleeding ankles and wrists.

About two weeks later, Shaw had to make an overnight trip. He dreaded leaving his wife and child alone. The words of the guard came back to him, and he was concerned about the safety of his family. When Shaw's wife went to the front door the morning she was alone, she was startled to see the three criminals lying on her steps. One of them explained, "We know the doctor go. We stay here all night so no harm come to you."

Even dangerous men are capable of responding to an act of love! Touched lives are the most important monuments you can leave.

THERE IS NO POVERTY THAT CAN OVERTAKE DILIGENCE.

He becometh poor that dealeth with a slack hand:
but the hand of the diligent maketh rich.
Proverbs 10:4

A young reporter once interviewed a successful business-man. The reporter asked the man to give him a detailed history of his company. As the man talked at length, the reporter began to be amazed by the great many problems the man had overcome. He finally asked him, "But how did you find the strength to overcome so much?"

The old gentleman leaned back in his chair and said, "There's really no trick to it." Then he added, "You know, there are some troubles that seem so high you can't climb over them." The reporter nodded in agreement, thinking of several he was currently facing. "And," the wise business-man went on, "there are some troubles so wide you can't walk around them." Again, the reporter nodded. The man went on, raising his voice dramatically, "And there are some problems so deep you can't dig under them." Eager for a solution, the reporter said, "Yes? Yes?"

"It's then," the man concluded, "that you know the only way to beat the problem is to duck your head and wade right through it."

A problem rarely decreases in size while a person stands and stares at it. But when you diligently pursue a solution, your problem is guaranteed to shrink.

NEVER DESPAIR; BUT IF YOU DO, WORK ON IN DESPAIR.

As for you, be strong and do not give up,
for your work will be rewarded.
2 Chronicles 15:7 NIV

American sports fans watched in awe on Sunday, March 4, 1979, as Phil took to the giant-slalom slopes at Whiteface Mountain, New York. He exploded onto the course and then settled into a powerful carving of the mountainside.

Nonetheless, at gate thirty-five, tragedy struck. Phil hooked his inside ski on a pole, went flying head over heels, and crashed in a crumpled heap. The ski team physician described the injury as "the ultimate broken ankle"—a break of both the ankle and lower leg. He had to put the bones back together with a three-inch metal plate and seven screws.

The question was not whether Phil would ever ski again but if he would ever walk again. Looking back, Phil describes the months after his injury as a time of deep despair. Still, he never entertained doubts about walking or skiing.

After two months on crutches and a high-disciplined exercise program, he forced himself to walk without limping. In August, he began skiing gentle slopes. Less than six months after the accident, he entered a race in Australia and finished second. In February of 1980, less than a year after his agonizing injury, Phil Mahre took on the same mountain where he had fallen. This time, he won an Olympic silver medal.

When defeat and despair threaten to overtake you and squash your dreams, keep on going. Eventually, you will overtake defeat with victory and despair with joy!

139

YOU CAN ACCOMPLISH MORE IN ONE HOUR WITH GOD THAN ONE LIFETIME WITHOUT HIM.

With God all things are possible.
Matthew 19:26

CLASS OF
2001

The Lord appeared to a man named Ananias in a vision and asked him to undertake what Ananias must surely have perceived as a dangerous mission. He directed him to go to the house of a man named Judas, lay his hands on a man named Saul of Tarsus, and pray that he might receive his sight. Saul had been blinded while traveling to Damascus to persecute the Christians there, having the full intent of taking them captive to Jerusalem for trial, torture, and death. Even so, Ananias did as the Lord asked him, and within the hour, Saul's sight was restored.

According to Christian legend, Ananias was a simple cobbler who had no idea what happened to Saul after that day, or how he had changed the course of human history by obeying God in a simple act that was part of Saul's transformation into the Apostle Paul. As he lay on his deathbed, Ananias looked up toward heaven and whispered, "I haven't done much, Lord: a few shoes sewn, a few sandals stitched. But what more could be expected of a poor cobbler?"

The Lord spoke in Ananias' heart, "Don't worry, Ananias, about how much you have accomplished—or how little. You were there in the hour I needed you, and that is all that matters."

Being in the right place at the right time, even if it's only for one hour, can give you the opportunity to change history. In order to be there, you must simply listen and obey.

141

IF YOU DON'T STAND FOR SOMETHING, YOU'LL FALL FOR ANYTHING!

If you do not stand firm in your faith,
you will not stand at all.
Isaiah 7:9 NIV

142

Former President Harry S. Truman once remarked that no president of our nation has ever escaped abuse or even libel from the press. He noted that it was common to hear a president publicly called a traitor. Truman further concluded that the president who had not fought with Congress or the Supreme Court hadn't done his job.

What is true for an American president is also true for everyone else. No matter what position a person may hold on a particular organizational chart or strata of society, he or she will be opposed, ridiculed, and perhaps even challenged to fight from time to time. That is why no one should strive to win a popularity contest. Instead, each person should live by his or her convictions.

It's inevitable that you will be criticized or attacked at some point in your life. But collapsing from *fear* of an attack isn't inevitable. Stand firm in your faith, and the Lord will stand with you!

PERSEVERANCE IS
A GREAT ELEMENT
OF SUCCESS; IF YOU
ONLY KNOCK LONG
ENOUGH AND LOUD
ENOUGH AT THE GATE,
YOU ARE SURE TO
WAKE UP SOMEBODY.

Ask, and it shall be given you; seek, and ye shall
find; knock, and it shall be opened unto you.
Luke 11:9

CLASS OF
2001

Country-music star Randy Travis and his manager, Lib, remember the lean days of his career—all 3,650 of them.

For ten years, Lib did whatever it took to keep her club open long enough for somebody to discover Travis' talent. For his part, Randy sang his heart out, and when he wasn't singing, he fried catfish or washed dishes in the kitchen. Then it happened. Everything seemed to click for him. He had a hit called "On the Other Hand," an album contract, a tour offer, and a movie deal. He was hot! Everyone seemed to be calling him an overnight success.

Travis notes, "We were turned down more than once by every label in Nashville. But I'm kind of one to believe that if you work at something long enough and keep believing, sooner or later it will happen."

In many instances in life, it's perseverance that makes the difference, but as the popular phrase states, you can "hang in there." Don't stop believing! Don't give up hope! Eventually the door will be opened.

145

MAN CANNOT DISCOVER NEW OCEANS UNLESS HE HAS THE COURAGE TO LOSE SIGHT OF THE SHORE.

*Peter got out of the boat, and walked
on the water and came toward Jesus.
Matthew 14:29 NAS*

It may seem easy to play it safe, but that isn't the way to build an exhilarating and fulfilled life. Playing life's game to the fullest requires taking calculated, informed risks. Without risk, life has little excitement or emotion. Soon it becomes dull and joyless. Consider this:

- To laugh is to risk appearing the fool.
- To weep is to risk appearing sentimental.
- To reach out for another is to risk involvement.
- To expose feelings is to risk exposing one's true self.
- To place ideas and dreams before a crowd is to risk ridicule.
- To love is to risk not being loved in return.
- To live is to risk dying.
- To hope is to risk despair.
- To try is to risk failure.

Yet the person who risks nothing, does nothing, has nothing, and ultimately becomes nothing. Don't be afraid to go for it.

CONSIDER THE POSTAGE STAMP: ITS USEFULNESS CONSISTS OF THE ABILITY TO STICK TO ONE THING TILL IT GETS THERE.

*I have fought a good fight, I have finished
my course, I have kept the faith.*
2 Timothy 4:7

In March of 1987, Eamon Coughlan was running in a qualifying heat at the World Indoor Track Championships in Indianapolis. The Irishman was the reigning world-record-holder at fifteen-hundred meters, and he was favored to win the race handily. Unfortunately, with two-and-a-half laps left to run, he was tripped and fell hard. Even so, he got up and with great effort, managed to catch the race leaders. With only twenty yards to go, he was in third place, which would have been good enough to qualify for the final race.

Then Coughlan looked over his shoulder to the inside. Seeing no one there, he relaxed his effort slightly. What he hadn't noticed, however, was that a runner was charging hard on the outside. This runner passed Coughlan just a yard before the finish line, thus eliminating him from the finals. Coughlan's great comeback effort ended up being worthless for one and only one reason, he momentarily took his eyes off the finish line and focused on the would-be competitors instead.

One of the most important factors in reaching your goals in life is to have a single-minded focus. Don't let yourself become distracted by what others do or say. Run your race to win!

149

IT NEEDS MORE SKILL THAN I CAN TELL TO PLAY THE SECOND FIDDLE WELL.

*He that is greatest among
you shall be your servant.
Matthew 23:11*

People often think of heart surgeons as being the arrogant prima donnas of the medical world. But those who know Dr. William DeVries, the surgeon who pioneered the artificial heart, couldn't *disagree* more. Co-workers at Humana Hospital Audubon in Louisville, Kentucky, describe DeVries as the kind of doctor who shows up on Sundays just to cheer up discouraged patients. He occasionally changes dressings, traditionally considered a nurse's job, and if a patient wants him to stick around and talk, he always does.

Friends say DeVries is an "old shoe" who fits in wherever he goes. He likes to wear cowboy boots with his surgical scrubs, and he often repairs hearts to the beat of Vivaldi or jazz. "He has always got a smile lurking," says Louisville cardiologist Dr. Robert Goodin. "And he's always looking for a way to let it out."

No matter how high you rise, never forget that you started at ground zero. Even if you were born to great wealth and privilege, you still were once a helpless babe. Real success comes not in thinking you have arrived at a place where others should serve you but in recognizing that in whatever place you are, you have arrived at a position where you can serve others.

CLASS OF 2001

151

A MAN NEVER DISCLOSES HIS OWN CHARACTER SO CLEARLY AS WHEN HE DESCRIBES ANOTHER'S.

*A good man out of the good treasure of the heart
bringeth forth good things: and an evil man out
of the evil treasure bringeth forth evil things.*
Matthew 12:35

After several months of romance, Napoleon and Josephine decided to marry. The notary who made out the marriage contract was one of Josephine's friends. He secretly advised her against marrying "an obscure little officer who has nothing besides his uniform and sword and has no future." He thought she should find someone of greater worth. With her charms, he advised, she might attract a wealthy man, perhaps an army contractor or a business investor.

Napoleon was in the next room while the notary was giving this advice to his beloved. He could hear every word that was said. Still, he did not disclose he had overheard. Years later, however, he had his revenge.

After his coronation as Emperor, this same notary appeared before him on a matter of business. At the conclusion of their appointment, Napoleon smiled and observed that Madame de Beauharnais—queen of France—had done very well, after all, to have married that "obscure little officer who possessed nothing besides his uniform and sword and had no future."

The notary was forced to agree that Madame, indeed, had done well. As for himself, he was still a notary!

Be careful before you pass judgment on another. You're revealing something about yourself, and your words may come back to bite you.

THE GREATEST USE OF LIFE IS TO SPEND IT FOR SOMETHING THAT WILL OUTLIVE YOU.

"Store up for yourselves treasures in heaven,
where moth and rust do not destroy, and
where thieves do not break in and steal."
Matthew 6:20 NIV

Although we do not have the original manuscripts of the New Testament, we do have more than 99.9 percent of the original text because of the faithful work of manuscript copyists over the centuries.

Copying was a long, arduous process. In ancient days, copyists did not sit at desks while writing, but rather stood or made copies while sitting on benches or stools, holding a scroll on their knees. Notes at the end of some scrolls tell of the drudgery of the work:

- "He who does not know how to write supposes it to be no labor; but though only three fingers write, the whole body labors."
- "Writing bows one's back, thrusts the ribs into one's stomach, and fosters a general debility."
- "As travelers rejoice to see their home country, so also is the end of a book to those who toil."

Even so, without the work of faithful copyists, we would not have the Scriptures today. As one scribe aptly noted: "There is no scribe who will not pass away, but what his hands have written will remain forever."

When you are choosing what you will do as your life's work, there are many things to consider. Don't underestimate the satisfaction that comes from knowing what you do today will touch lives long after you are gone.

CLASS OF 2001

EVERY MAN'S WORK,
WHETHER IT BE
LITERATURE, OR
MUSIC, OR PICTURES,
OR ARCHITECTURE,
OR ANYTHING ELSE,
IS ALWAYS A PORTRAIT
OF HIMSELF.

As in water face reflects face,
So the heart of man reflects man.
Proverbs 27:19 NAS

A young man once made an appointment with a well-published author. The first question the author asked him was, "Why did you want to see me?"

The young man stammered, "Well, I'm a writer, too. I was hoping you could share with me some of your secrets for successful writing."

The author asked a second question, "What have you written?"

"Nothing," the young man replied, "at least nothing that is finished yet."

The author asked a third question, "Well, if you haven't written anything, then tell me, what are you writing?"

The young man replied, "Well, I'm in school right now, so I'm not writing anything at present."

The author then asked a fourth question, "So why do you call yourself a writer?"

Writers write. Composers compose. Painters paint. Workmen work. What you do to a great extent defines who you are and what you become. What does your work say about you? When your work on the outside is in harmony with who you are on the inside, you have found your true purpose in life.

157

WHAT WE DO ON SOME
GREAT OCCASION
WILL PROBABLY
DEPEND ON WHAT
WE ALREADY ARE;
AND WHAT WE ARE
WILL BE THE RESULT
OF PRECIOUS YEARS
OF SELF-DISCIPLINE.

*I keep under my body, and
bring it into subjection.*
1 Corinthians 9:27

CLASS OF
2001

During a homecoming football game against rival Concordia, Augsburg College found itself losing miserably. But late in the fourth quarter, nose guard David Stevens came off the bench and sparked a fire. He initiated or assisted in two tackles, and when a Concordia player fumbled the ball, David fell on it. As he held the recovered ball high, the crowd roared. It was an unforgettable moment for Augsburg fans!

David Lee Stevens was born to a woman who had taken thalidomide, an anti-nausea drug given to many pregnant women in the early '60s. To the horror of many parents and physicians, it was soon clear that the drug causes severe birth defects. David's feet appeared where his legs should have started.

Abandoned by his mother, David was adopted by a foster family. Bee and Bill Stevens imposed strict rules of behavior on David, nurtured him, and loved him. They insisted he learn to do things for himself, and they never put him in a wheelchair. At age three, he was fitted with "legs."

In school, David became a student leader, made good grades, organized special events, and befriended new students. In high school, he not only played football, but baseball, basketball, and hockey. He became a champion wrestler. When offered handicap license plates, he refused them stating simply, "Those are for people who need them. I am not 'disabled.'"

David was taught to discipline himself, and so he was able to perform, in spite of his apparent handicap. Whatever obstacle may be in your way, self-discipline can help you either rise above it or plow right through it.

OUR DEEDS DETERMINE US, AS MUCH AS WE DETERMINE OUR DEEDS.

Even a child is known by his actions,
by whether his conduct is pure and right.
Proverbs 20:11 NIV

God's Little Devotional Book

In the fourth round of a national spelling bee in Washington, eleven-year-old Rosalie Elliot, a champion from South Carolina, was asked to spell the word *avowal*. Her soft Southern accent made it difficult for the judges to determine if she had used an *a* or an *e* as the next to last letter of the word. They deliberated for several minutes and also listened to tape-recorded playbacks, but they still couldn't determine which letter had been pronounced.

Finally the chief judge, John Lloyd, put the question to the only person who knew the answer. He asked Rosalie, "Was the letter an *a* or an *e*?"

Rosalie, surrounded by whispering young spellers, knew by now the correct spelling of the word. But without hesitation, she replied that she had misspelled the word and had used an *e*.

As she walked from the stage, the entire audience stood and applauded her honesty and integrity, including dozens of newspaper reporters covering the event. While Rosalie had not won the contest, she had definitely come out a winner that day.

We often think that who we are determines what we do. It is equally true that what you do today will determine, in part, who you become tomorrow.

161

ALL VIRTUE IS SUMMED UP IN DEALING JUSTLY.

He hath shewed thee, O man, what is good;
and what doth the LORD require of thee,
but to do justly, and to love mercy,
and to walk humbly with thy God?
Micah 6:8

CLASS OF
2001

To crack the lily-white system of higher education in Georgia in the 1960s, black leaders decided they needed to find only two "squeaky-clean" students who couldn't be challenged on moral, intellectual, or educational grounds.

In a discussion about who might be chosen, Alfred Holmes immediately volunteered his son, Hamilton, the top black male senior in the city. Charlayne Hunter-Fault also stepped forward and expressed an interest in applying to the university. Georgia delayed admitting both boys on grounds it had no room in its dormitories, and the matter eventually ended up in federal court. Judge Bootle ordered the university to admit the two, who were qualified in every respect. Thus, segregation ended at the university level in that state, and soon, the nation.

Attorney General Robert Kennedy declared in a speech not long after: "We know that it is the law which enables men to live together, that creates order out of chaos. And we know that if one man's rights are denied, the rights of all are endangered."

Justice may be universal, but it always begins at the individual level.

163

NO MATTER WHAT A MAN'S PAST MAY HAVE BEEN, HIS FUTURE IS SPOTLESS.

Forgetting those things which are behind, and reaching forth unto those things which are before.
Philippians 3:13

164

Willingway Hospital is one of the nation's top treatment centers for alcoholism and drug addiction. There would be no Willingway, however, if it weren't for Dot and John, who at one time seemed the least likely candidates to found such a hospital.

Early in their courtship, Dot and John drank heavily, and after they married, they began taking amphetamines. John, a medical doctor, was arrested for writing himself narcotics prescriptions. He spent six months in prison, eventually falling on his knees and crying out to God to help him overcome his addictions.

When John returned to medical practice drug-free and alcohol-free, he began to receive referrals from other doctors to treat their alcoholic patients. Dot and John set up three beds under the chandelier in their own dining room as a detox room. Among their patients have been three of their own four children.

As word of their compassion spread, they established a forty-bed hospital on eleven acres close to their home. The chandelier still hangs in the detox room as a symbol of hope. All four children have worked on the medical or administrative staff of Willingway.

Regardless of your past, your future is yet to be written. With God's help, your mistakes can be your greatest assets.

CLASS OF 2001

ONE OF LIFE'S GREAT RULES IS THIS: THE MORE YOU GIVE, THE MORE YOU GET.

*"Whatever measure you use in giving—
large or small—it will be used to
measure what is given back to you."*
Luke 6:38 NLT

CLASS OF
2001

Three young men were each given three kernels of corn by a wise old sage, who admonished them to go out into the world and use the corn to bring themselves good fortune.

The first young man put his three kernels of corn into a bowl of hot broth and ate them. The second thought, *I can do better than that!* He planted his three kernels of corn. Within a few months, he had three stalks of corn. He took the ears of corn from the stalks, boiled them, and had enough corn for three meals.

The third man said to himself, *I can do better than that!* He also planted his three kernels of corn, but when his three stalks of corn grew and matured, he stripped one of the ears and replanted all of the seeds, gave the second ear of corn to a sweet maiden, and ate the third. His one full ear's worth of replanted corn kernels gave him 200 stalks of corn! He planted the kernels from these stalks, setting aside only a small amount to eat.

Using this method, he eventually had one-hundred acres of corn. With his fortune, he not only won the hand of the sweet maiden but also purchased the land owned by the sweet maiden's father. He never hungered again.

If you want to receive in life, you must first learn to give.

167

EVERYTHING COMES TO HIM WHO HUSTLES WHILE HE WAITS.

We do not want you to become lazy,
but to imitate those who through faith and
patience inherit what has been promised.
Hebrews 6:12 NIV

168

In 1928, a happy, ambitious young nursing student was diagnosed with tuberculosis. Her family sent her to a nursing home in Saranac Lake for several months of "curing." She would remain in bed for twenty-one years! Most people may have given up, but not Isabel Smith. She approached the threshold of death on several occasions, but she never ceased to pursue the art of living. She read voraciously, loved to write letters, studied geography, and taught other patients to read and write. From her bed, she studied atomic energy with a fellow patient, a young physicist, and organized a town hall on the topic.

While ill, she met a kind, gentleman, who was also a patient at the sanitarium. She dreamed of marrying him and having a little house "under the mountains." At her lowest ebb, her dream kept her going, and in 1948, they did marry. She then wrote a book about "all the good things life has brought me." *Wish I Might,* published in 1955, earned her enough in royalties to buy her mountain retreat.

A tragic life? Hardly! Isabel Smith achieved everything she set out to achieve. She could have been content to lie there in her sickbed waiting for her cure. Instead, she fervently pursued her interests and made a life for herself.

169

GOD HAS NOTHING TO SAY TO THE SELF-RIGHTEOUS.

We have believed in Christ Jesus,
that we might be accepted by God
because of our faith in Christ. . . . For no
one will ever be saved by obeying the law.
Galatians 2:16 NLT

According to an old legend, two monks named Tanzan and Ekido were traveling together down a muddy road. Heavy monsoon rains had saturated the area, and they were grateful for a few moments of sunshine to make their journey. Before long, they came around a bend and encountered a lovely girl in a silk kimono. She looked extremely forlorn as she stared at the muddy road before her.

At once, Tanzan responded to her plight. "Come here, girl," he said. Then lifting her in his arms, he carried her over the slippery ooze and set her down on the other side of the road.

As they went on their way, Tanzan noticed that Ekido was uncharacteristically silent. It was apparent that something was bothering him deeply, but try as he would, Tanzan couldn't get Ekido to talk to him. Then that night after they reached their intended lodging, Ekido could no longer restrain his anger and disappointment. "We monks don't go near females," he said to Tanzan in an accusing voice. "We especially don't go near young and lovely maidens. It is dangerous. Why did you do that?"

"I left the girl back there, Ekido," replied Tanzan. "Are you still carrying her?"

God is not pleased when we practice the letter of the law without regard for the spirit behind it. Christ has established a new law—the law of love. That should always be our model for right living.

CLASS OF
2001

DEFEAT IS NOT THE WORST OF FAILURES. NOT TO HAVE TRIED IS THE TRUE FAILURE.

Be strong and of a good courage; be not afraid,
neither be thou dismayed: for the LORD thy
God is with thee withersoever thou goest.
Joshua 1:9

There once was a young man who lived a most miserable life. Orphaned before he was three, he was taken in by strangers. He was kicked out of school, suffered from poverty, and as the result of inherited physical weaknesses, he developed serious heart trouble as a teenager. His beloved wife died early in their marriage. He lived as an invalid most of his adult life, and he eventually died at the young age of forty. By all outward appearances, he lived a life doomed to defeat and obscurity.

Even so, he never quit trying to express himself and achieve success. During a twenty-year period, he produced some of the most brilliant articles, essays, and criticisms ever written. His poetry is still read widely and studied by virtually every high school student in the United States. His short stories and detective stories are well known. One of his poems, on display at the famous Huntington library in California, has been valued at more than fifty-thousand dollars, which is far more than the young man earned in his entire lifetime.

His name? Edgar Allan Poe.

Circumstances don't affect your chances for success nearly as much as your level of effort!

UNLESS YOU TRY TO DO SOMETHING BEYOND WHAT YOU HAVE ALREADY MASTERED, YOU WILL NEVER GROW.

Reaching forth unto those things which are before, I press toward the mark for the prize of the high calling of God in Christ Jesus.
Philippians 3:13-14

After falling twice in the 1988 Olympic speed-skating races, Dan Jansen sought out sports psychologist Dr. Jim Loehr, who helped him find a new balance between his sport and his life. He also helped Jansen learn to focus on the mental aspects of skating.

Peter Mueller became his coach, putting him through workouts that Dan has since described as the "toughest I've ever known." By the time the 1994 Olympics arrived, Jansen had more confidence than ever. He had set a five-hundred-meter world record just two months earlier. The Olympic title in that event seemed to belong to him!

Unfortunately, Jansen fell during the five-hundred-meter race. He was disappointed and shaken, but Dr. Loehr immediately advised, "Start preparing for the one thousand-meter race. The five-hundred-meter is gone. Put it behind you."

The problem was that the one-thousand-meter was Jansen's weakest event. He had always felt he could not win at that distance. Now it was his last chance for an Olympic medal. As the race began, Jansen said, "I just seemed to be sailing along," and then he slipped and came within an inch of stepping on a lane marker. Still, he resisted the urge to panic and raced on, attaining a world-record time that won him the gold medal!

It's a safe feeling to stick with those areas you have mastered and feel confident about. But if you stay there, you will not grow. Seek out opportunities to master new skills and reach new goals. Don't be intimidated! With a strong mental attitude, your weakest event can become your greatest triumph.

CLASS OF
2001

175

I DON'T KNOW THE SECRET TO SUCCESS, BUT THE KEY TO FAILURE IS TO TRY TO PLEASE EVERYONE.

*Am I now trying to win the
approval of men, or of God?
Galatians 1:10 NIV*

A young man once studied violin under a world-renowned violinist and master teacher. For several years, he worked hard perfecting his talent. The day finally came when he was called upon to give his first major public recital in the large city where both he and his teacher lived.

Following each selection, which he performed with great skill and passion, the performer seemed uneasy about the great applause he received. Even though he knew that those in the audience were musically astute and not likely to give such applause for anything less than a superior performance, the young man acted almost as if he couldn't hear the appreciation that was being showered upon him.

At the close of the last number, the applause was thunderous and numerous "Bravos" were shouted. But the talented young violinist had his eyes glued on one spot only. Finally, when an elderly man in the first row of the balcony smiled and nodded to him in approval, the young man relaxed and beamed with both relief and joy. His teacher had praised his work! The applause of thousands meant nothing until he had first won the approval of the master.

Who are you trying to please today? You will never be able to please everyone, but you can please the One who matters most—your Father God. Keep your eyes on Him, and you can't fail.

CLASS OF 2001

177

KITES RISE HIGHEST AGAINST THE WIND, NOT WITH IT.

When the way is rough, your patience has a chance to grow. So let it grow, and don't try to squirm out of your problems.
James 1:3-4 TLB

The engineers hired to build a suspension bridge across the Niagara River faced a serious problem: how to get the first cable from one side of the river to the other. The river was too wide to throw the cable to the other side and too swift to cross by boat.

An engineer finally came up with a solution! With a favoring stiff wind, a kite was lofted and allowed to drift over the river and land on the opposite shore. Attached to the kite was a light string, which was threaded through the kite's tip so that both ends of the string were in the hands of the kite flyer. Once the kite was in the hand of engineers on the far side, they removed the kite from its string and set up a pulley. A small rope was attached to one end of the original kite string and pulled across the river. At the end of this string, a piece of rope was attached and pulled across and so on, until a cable strong enough to sustain the iron cable, which supported the bridge, could be drawn across the water.

Let your faith soar like that kite! Release it to God, believing that He can and will help you. When you link your released faith with patience and persistence, you will have what it takes to tackle virtually any problem.

THE SECRET OF SUCCESS IS TO BE LIKE A DUCK— SMOOTH AND UNRUFFLED ON TOP, BUT PADDLING FURIOUSLY UNDERNEATH.

His peace will keep your thoughts and your hearts quiet and at rest as you trust in Christ Jesus.
Philippians 4:7 TLB

CLASS OF 2001

Ellen Burstyn, a Tony Award-winning actress, once had a memorable acting lesson that she enjoys relating to those who question her about stage fright:

> One day on Broadway, I became aware of a stir in the audience. Suddenly, I saw it! A stray cat was nonchalantly crossing the stage.
>
> The cat stopped and turned toward the darkness of the audience and seemed startled to discover that the darkness was alive. She had presence, as though there were a thousand pairs of eyes out there, which, of course, there were. That realization stopped the cat dead in her tracks. Then she fled into the wings. I remember thinking, *I know just how she feels.*
>
> I've often told this story to young actors because I think it shows that the job of the actor is to make contact with the kitty inside each of us—the one that wants to turn and run when it feels those thousand pairs of eyes on it. And to find the way to quiet the kitty and just go on doing what we have to do.[6]

Feeling frightened or nervous is not a sign of impending failure. It is a sign that you consider the performance ahead to be worth doing and doing well! Keep your eyes on your goal and remember those who will benefit from your work. This focus will calm your fears and fill you with purpose.

CLASS OF 2001

181

THE CHEERFUL MAN WILL DO MORE IN THE SAME TIME, WILL DO IT BETTER, WILL PRESERVE IT LONGER, THAN THE SAD OR SULLEN.

*When a man is gloomy, everything
seems to go wrong; when he is
cheerful, everything seems right!*
Proverbs 15:15 TLB

A little boy was once overheard talking to himself as he strutted out of his house into the backyard, carrying a baseball bat and ball. Once in the yard, he tipped his baseball cap to his eager puppy, and picking up the bat and ball, he announced with a loud voice, "I'm the greatest hitter in the world."

He then proceeded to toss the ball into the air, swing at it, and miss. "Strike one!" he cried, as if playing the role of umpire.

The boy picked up the ball, threw it into the air, and said again, "I'm the greatest baseball hitter ever!" Again he swung at the ball and missed. "Strike two!" he announced to his dog and the yard.

Undaunted, he picked up the ball, examined his bat, and then just before tossing the ball into the air, announced once again, "I'm the greatest hitter who ever lived." He swung the bat hard, but missed the ball for the third time. "Strike three!" he cried. Then he added, "Wow! What a pitcher! I'm the greatest pitcher in all the world!"

An upbeat, positive mental attitude paves the way for a productive and satisfying life.

MONEY IS A GOOD SERVANT BUT A BAD MASTER.

The rich ruleth over the poor, and
the borrower is servant to the lender.
Proverbs 22:7

184

At the age of twenty-four, financial advisor and author Ron Blue felt he had everything he needed to be successful—an MBA degree, a CPA certificate, and a prestigious position in the New York City office of the world's largest CPA firm. But then at the age of thirty-two, he committed his life to Jesus Christ and gained a new perspective.

When Blue decided to establish his own financial advisory firm, he used his skills to develop a business plan and arrange for a ten-thousand-dollar line of credit at a bank. Almost immediately, however, he felt convicted that God did not want him to borrow money to start his business. He canceled the credit line, not knowing what to do next but knowing he was not to go into debt.

One day, while explaining his business idea to a friend, the friend said, "Would you consider designing a financial seminar for our executives who are getting ready to retire?" Ron jumped at the opportunity. His friend was the training director for a large company, and the company agreed to pay six thousand dollars in advance for development of the seminar, then one thousand dollars each for four seminars during the year. Ron had the ten thousand dollars he needed without borrowing a dime.

Do your best to stay out of debt. You'll feel much freer, and God will bless you for trusting in Him.

CLASS OF
2001

NO PLAN IS WORTH THE PAPER IT IS PRINTED ON UNLESS IT STARTS YOU DOING SOMETHING.

Be ye doers of the word, and not hearers only, deceiving your own selves.
James 1:22

Nelson Diebel, a hyperactive and delinquent child, was enrolled in the Peddie School where he met swimming coach Christ Martin, who believed the more one practices, the better one performs. Within a month, he had Nelson swimming thirty to forty hours a week, even though Nelson could not sit still in a classroom for fifteen minutes.

Martin saw potential in Nelson. He constantly put new goals in front of the boy, trying to get him to focus and turn his anger into strength. Nelson eventually qualified for the Junior Nationals, and from there, the Olympic trials.

Then disaster struck. Nelson broke both hands and arms in a diving accident, and doctors warned he probably would never regain his winning form. Martin said to him, "You're coming all the way back. If you're not committed to that, we're going to stop right now." Nelson agreed, and within weeks after his casts were off, he was swimming again.

In 1992, Nelson Diebel won an Olympic gold medal. As he accepted his medal, he recalls thinking: *I planned and dreamed and worked so hard and I did it!* The kid who once couldn't sit still and who had no ambition had learned to make a plan, pursue it, and achieve it. He had become a winner in far more than swimming!

Dream big dreams! Then establish a plan, and stick with it! The possibilities are limitless.

LIFE IS A COIN. YOU CAN SPEND IT ANY WAY YOU WISH, BUT YOU CAN SPEND IT ONLY ONCE.

It is appointed unto men once to die,
but after this the judgment.
Hebrews 9:27

Frank, the head and founder of a major contracting firm, refused to celebrate the holidays, saying only, "Christmas is for children." Then one brisk December day, as Frank was walking to work he was drawn to a Nativity scene in a department store window. That day, he saw the Child anew.

As Frank started to move away from the window, a sign across the street caught his attention: "Holy Innocents Home." His mind raced back to a Sunday school lesson years ago about how King Herod had feared the Baby Jesus and slaughtered children in Bethlehem. He recalled the day his own son, David, had died at the age of eighteen months. He had not been able to speak his name since.

Impulsively, Frank visited the library and was surprised to learn that Herod's men were estimated to have killed twenty children. He left the library with a mission. Later that night, he told his wife, Adele, that he had visited the orphanage and given money for the building of a new wing. Then he said, "They are going to name it for David."

What Frank did not tell his wife was that he had had a vision of twenty children playing in a bright new wing at Holy Innocents. As Adele hugged him, the vision came again, but this time, there were twenty-one children at play.

Don't miss the opportunity to spend your life on something worthwhile. You may have several opportunities, some big and some small, but none of them will be insignificant.

ONLY PASSIONS, GREAT PASSIONS, CAN ELEVATE THE SOUL TO GREAT THINGS.

Fervent in spirit; serving the Lord.
Romans 12:11

CLASS OF 2001

The German sculptor, Dannaker, worked for two years on a statue of Christ until it looked perfect to him. He called a little girl into his studio, and pointing to the statue, he asked her, "Who is that?" The little girl promptly replied, "A great man."

Dannaker was disheartened. He took his chisel and began anew. For six long years, he toiled. Again, he invited a little girl into his workshop, stood her before the figure, and said, "Who is that?" She looked up at it for a moment, and then tears welled up in her eyes as she folded her hands across her chest and said, "Suffer the little children to come unto me" (Mark 10:14). This time Dannaker knew he had succeeded.

The sculptor later confessed that during those six years, Christ had revealed Himself to him in a vision, and he had only transferred to the marble what he had seen with his inner eyes.

Later, when Napoleon Bonaparte asked him to make a statue of Venus for the Louvre, Dannaker refused. "A man," he said, "who had seen Christ can never employ his gifts in carving a pagan goddess. My art is henceforth a consecrated thing."

The true value of a work comes not from effort, nor its completion, but from Christ who inspires it.

FAILURES WANT PLEASING METHODS, SUCCESSES WANT PLEASING RESULTS.

No discipline seems pleasant at the time,
but painful. Later on, however, it produces
a harvest of righteousness and peace
for those who have been trained by it.
Hebrews 12:11 NIV

Sadie Delaney's father taught her always to strive to do better than her competition. She proved the value of that lesson shortly before she received her teaching license. A supervisor came to watch her and two other student teachers. Their assignment was to teach a class to bake cookies. Since the supervisor didn't have time for each teacher to go through the entire lesson, she divided the lesson, and Sadie was assigned to teach the girls how to serve and clean up.

The first student teacher panicked and forgot to halve the recipe and preheat the oven. The second girl was so behind because of the first girl's errors that the students made a mess in forming and baking the cookies. Then it was Sadie's turn. She said to the girls, "Listen, we have to work as a team."

They quickly baked the remaining dough. Several girls were lined up to scrub pans as soon as the cookies came out of the oven. Within ten minutes, they had several dozen perfect cookies and a clean kitchen. The supervisor was so impressed, she offered Sadie a substitute teacher's license on the spot. Sadie soon became the first black person ever to teach domestic science in New York City's public high schools.

Even when you have every right to blame others who have gone before you, don't make excuses. Do what it takes to get the job done!

CLASS OF 2001

193

ONCE A WORD HAS BEEN ALLOWED TO ESCAPE, IT CANNOT BE RECALLED.

Let no corrupt communication proceed out of your mouth, but that which is good to the use of edifying, that it may minister grace unto the hearers.
Ephesians 4:29

194

CLASS OF
2001

A man once sat down to have dinner with his family. Before they began to eat, the family members joined hands around the table, and the man said a prayer, thanking God for the food, the hands that had prepared it, and for the Source of all life. During the meal, however, he complained at length about the staleness of the bread, the bitterness of the coffee, and a bit of mold he found on one edge of the brick of cheese.

His young daughter asked him, "Daddy, do you think God heard you say grace before the meal?"

"Of course, honey," he answered confidently.

Then she asked, "Do you think God heard everything that was said during dinner?" The man answered, "Why, yes, I believe so. God hears everything."

She thought for a moment and then asked, "Daddy, which do you think God believed?"

The Lord hears everything we say during a day, not only those words that are addressed specifically to Him. Once you've said something, you can't take it back. Would you mind if God listened in on your conversations?

MOST OF THE THINGS WORTH DOING IN THE WORLD WERE DECLARED IMPOSSIBLE BEFORE THEY WERE DONE.

With God all things are possible.
Matthew 19:26

Consider these examples of resistance to ideas and inventions that we now consider commonplace:

- In Germany, experts proved that if trains went as fast as fifteen miles an hour—considered a frightful speed—blood would spurt from the travelers' noses and passengers would suffocate when going through tunnels. In the United States, experts said the introduction of the railroad would require the building of many insane asylums, since people would be driven mad with terror at the sight of the locomotives.

- The New York YWCA announced typing lessons for women in 1881, and vigorous protest erupted on the grounds that the female constitution would break down under the strain.

- When the idea of iron ships was proposed, experts insisted that they would not float, that they would damage more easily than wooden ships when grounding, that it would be difficult to preserve the iron bottom from rust, and that iron would play havoc with compass readings.

- New Jersey farmers resisted the first successful cast-iron plow invented in 1797, claiming that the cast iron would poison the land and stimulate the growth of weeds.

Don't let the word *impossible* stop you. If inventors and visionaries left every impossible task undone, our lives would be considerably more difficult. Nothing worth doing is impossible with the help of God!

OBSTACLES ARE THOSE FRIGHTFUL THINGS YOU SEE WHEN YOU TAKE YOUR EYES OFF THE GOAL.

Peter . . . walked on the water toward Jesus.
But when he looked around at the high waves,
he was terrified and began to sink.
Matthew 14:29-30 TLB

During the darkest days of the Civil War, the hopes of the Union nearly died. When certain goals seemed unreachable, the leaders of the Union turned to President Abraham Lincoln for solace, guidance, and encouragement. Once when a delegation called at the White House and detailed a long list of crises facing the nation, Lincoln told this story:

> Years ago a young friend and I were out one night when a shower of meteors fell from the clear November sky. The young man was frightened, but I told him to look up in the sky past the shooting stars to the fixed stars beyond, shining serene in the firmament, and I said, "Let us not mind the meteors, but let us keep our eyes on the stars."

When times are troubled or life seems to be changing too fast, keep your inner eyes of faith and hope on those things that you know to be lasting and sure. Don't limit your gaze to what you know or who you know, but focus on whom you know. God alone—and a relationship with Him is the supreme goal. He never changes, and He cannot be removed from His place as the King of glory.

CLASS OF 2001

A GOOD REPUTATION IS MORE VALUABLE THAN MONEY.

A good name is rather to be chosen than great riches.
Proverbs 22:1

CLASS OF
2001

In *Up from Slavery,* Booker T. Washington describes meeting an ex-slave from Virginia:

> I found that this man had made a contract with his master two or three years previous to the Emancipation Proclamation. The slave was to be permitted to buy himself, by paying so much per year for his body; and while he was paying for himself, he was to be permitted to labor where and for whom he pleased. Finding that he could secure better wages in Ohio, he went there.
>
> When freedom came, the man was still in debt to his master some three hundred dollars. Notwithstanding that the Emancipation Proclamation freed him from any obligation to his master, this black man walked back to where his old master lived in Virginia, and placed the last dollar, with interest, in his hands.
>
> In talking to me about this, the man told me that he knew that he did not have to pay his debt, but that he had given his word to his master, and he had never broken his word. He felt that he could not enjoy his freedom till he had fulfilled his promise.

Your ability to keep your word, not your ability to acquire money, is your true measure as a person!

AN ERROR DOESN'T BECOME A MISTAKE UNTIL YOU REFUSE TO CORRECT IT.

He who heeds discipline shows the way to life, but whoever ignores correction leads others astray.
Proverbs 10:17 NIV

A janitor at the First Security Bank in Boise, Idaho, once accidentally put a box of eight-thousand checks worth eight hundred and forty thousand dollars on a trash table. That night, the operator of the paper shredder dutifully dumped the box of checks into his machine, which cut the checks into quarter-inch shreds. He then dumped the paper scraps into a garbage can outside the bank. When the bank supervisor realized what had happened, he wanted to cry.

Most of the checks had been cashed at the bank and were awaiting shipment to a clearinghouse. Their loss represented a bookkeeping nightmare, since most of the checks were still unrecorded. As a result, the bankers could not know who paid what to whom.

What did the supervisor do? He ordered that the shredded pieces be reconstructed. So fifty employees worked in two shifts for six hours a day inside six rooms—sorting, matching, and pasting the pieces together as if they were jigsaw puzzles—until all eight thousand of the checks were put together again.

Humpty Dumpty fell from the wall, and the king's men didn't even try to put him together again. If you make a mistake, work on a solution!

HATING PEOPLE IS LIKE BURNING DOWN YOUR OWN HOUSE TO GET RID OF A RAT.

If ye bite and devour one another, take heed
that ye be not consumed one of another.
Galatians 5:15

204

After two years in the navy, Willard Scott returned to his old job with NBC radio, but to a new supervisor. Willard found himself at odds with his new boss at every turn, and he was furious when he rescheduled "Joy Boys," a comedy show Willard did with Eddie Walker, for the worst slot on radio—eight to midnight.

Willard was braced for a "change-or-I'll-leave" confrontation when he recalled Proverbs 19:11—*A man's wisdom gives him patience; it is to his glory to overlook an offense* (NIV). He and Eddie decided to work themselves to the bone, and within three years, they made "Joy Boys" the top-rated show in Washington.

Willard says,

> I learned that I too had been wrong. In all my dealings with my boss, I had aggravated the problem. I knew he didn't like me, and in response, I was barely civil to him and dodged him as much as I could. But one day he invited me to a station party I couldn't avoid. There I met his fiancée. She was bright, alive, and down-to-earth. By talking to her, I was able to get new insight into my boss' character. As time went on, my attitude changed, and so did his.

Willard and his boss became friends, and he remained at NBC.

Is there someone with whom you are at odds? If you're looking for the negative qualities in a person, you're sure to find them. Try seeing that person in a different light. A fresh perspective can change everything.

LAUGHTER IS THE SUN THAT DRIVES WINTER FROM THE HUMAN FACE.

A merry heart maketh a cheerful countenance: but by sorrow of the heart the spirit is broken.
Proverbs 15:13

A missionary from Sweden was once urged by his friends to give up his idea of returning to India, because it was so hot there. "Man," the fellow Swede urged, as if telling his friend something he didn't already know, "it's 120 degrees in the shade in that country!" The Swedish missionary replied, "Vell, ve don't alvays have to stay in the shade do ve?"

Humor is not a sin. It is a God-given escape hatch. Being able to see the lighter side of life is a virtue. Every vocation and circumstance of life has a lighter side, if we are only willing to see it. Wholesome humor can do a great deal to help defuse a tense, heated situation. In developing a good sense of humor, we must be able to laugh at our own mistakes; accept justified criticism; and learn to avoid using statements that are unsuitable, even though they may be funny.

James M. Gray and William Houghton—two godly men—were praying together one day, and the elderly Dr. Gray concluded his prayer by saying, "Lord, keep me cheerful. Keep me from becoming a cranky, old man."

Keeping a sense of humor is a great way to become a sweet, patient, and encouraging person. Learn to laugh at yourself occasionally!

GOOD NATURE BEGETS SMILES, SMILES BEGET FRIENDS, AND FRIENDS ARE BETTER THAN A FORTUNE.

The light in the eyes [of him whose heart is joyful] rejoices the hearts of others.
Proverbs 15:30 AMP

It has been estimated that more than ninety-five percent of all Americans receive at least one or more Christmas cards each year. The average is actually more than seventy cards per family! Millions of cards are mailed worldwide each holiday season. Have you ever wondered where this custom began?

A museum director in the mid-nineteenth century had a personal habit of sending notes to his friends at Christmastime each year, just to wish them a joyful holiday season. One year, he found he had little time to write, and yet he still wanted to send a message of good cheer. He asked his friend, John Horsely, to design a card that he might sign and send. Those who received the cards loved them so much they created cards of their own. Thus the Christmas card was invented!

It's often the simple heartfelt gestures in life that speak of friendship. Ask yourself today, *What can I do to bring a smile to the face of a friend? What can I do to bring good cheer into the life of someone who is in need, trouble, sickness, or sorrow?* Follow-through on your answer. It's not a gift you are giving as much as a friendship you are building!

CLASS OF
2001

209

NO PERSON WAS EVER HONORED FOR WHAT HE RECEIVED. HONOR HAS BEEN THE REWARD FOR WHAT HE GAVE.

The righteous give without sparing.
Proverbs 21:26 NIV

CLASS OF
2001

An American received a medical degree from New York University College of Medicine and earned an appointment to the Virus Research Laboratory at the University of Pittsburgh. Among the many honors he received for his work was a Presidential Medal of Freedom.

However, Jonas Salk is not known for what he received but for what he gave. He and his team of researchers gave their efforts to prepare an inactivated polio virus that could serve as an immunizing agent against polio. By 1952 they had created a vaccine. And in 1955 the vaccine was released for widespread use in the United States, virtually ending the ravaging, crippling effects of polio.

You will receive many opportunities in your life, and most likely a number of certificates, diplomas, and awards. But what ultimately will count is what you do with the training you have received and the skills and traits you have developed.

Find a way to give, create, or generate something today that will benefit others. Your actions may or may not bring you fame, but they will certainly bring you a sense of personal satisfaction—the greatest reward of all.

THE DIFFERENCE BETWEEN THE RIGHT WORD AND THE ALMOST RIGHT WORD IS THE DIFFERENCE BETWEEN LIGHTNING AND THE LIGHTNING BUG.

*A word fitly spoken is like apples
of gold in pictures of silver.
Proverbs 25:11*

CLASS OF 2001

Consider the infamous statements listed below, and notice as you read that they all could be *corrected* by changing or inserting only one word!

- "Everything that can be invented has been invented."—Charles H. Duell, U.S. Patent Office direct, 1899.
- "Who wants to hear actors talk?"—H. M. Warner, Warner Brothers Pictures 1927.
- "Sensible and responsible women do not want to vote."—Grover Cleveland, 1905.
- "There is no likelihood man can ever tap the power of the atom"—Robert Millikan, Nobel Prize winner in physics, 1923.
- "Heavier-than-air flying machines are impossible"—Lord Kelvin, president, Royal Society, 1895.
- "[Babe] Ruth made a big mistake when he gave up pitching"—Tris Speaker, 1927.
- "*Gone with the Wind* is going to be the biggest flop in Hollywood history"—Gary Cooper.

Isn't it amazing what a difference a word or two can make! Choose your words carefully. Always think before you speak.

THIS WORLD BELONGS TO THE MAN WHO IS WISE ENOUGH TO CHANGE HIS MIND IN THE PRESENCE OF FACTS.

Whoever heeds correction gains understanding.
Proverbs 15:32 NIV

A feud developed between two families who lived side by side in the mountains of Kentucky. It started when Grandpa Smith's cow jumped a stone fence and ate Grandpa Brown's corn. Brown shot the cow. A Smith boy then shot *two* Brown boys. The Browns shot one Smith. Bill Brown planned to kill a second Smith, but before he could, he was called away to war. While he was away, Bill's mother had a hard time making ends meet for her family, since Bill's father had been one of the victims.

At Christmas, the head of the Smith clan took his family to church. Usually he stayed outside, but this year it was so cold he went in to wait. The sermon was on Christ, the Prince of peace, who died in *our* place for *our* sins. It struck him hard. He realized what a crime he had committed, repented, and then secretly hired a young boy to carry a basket of food to the Brown's home every day until Bill returned.

Once home, Bill set out to discover who had so generously helped his family. He followed the boy to the Smith's house, where Smith met him and said, "Shoot me, Bill, if you want to. But Christ has already died for my sins, and I hope you'll forgive me, too." Bill did, and the neighbors truly became neighbors again.

Never reach the point in life where you think you can't learn something new, or change your opinion about something. You are never too old, or too young, to be forgiven.

GOOD WORDS ARE WORTH MUCH AND COST LITTLE.

Reprove, rebuke, exhort, with
great patience and instruction.
2 Timothy 4:2 NAS

216

One day a young altar boy was serving the priest at a Sunday Mass being held in the country church of his small village. The boy, nervous in his new role at the altar, accidentally dropped the cruet of wine. The village priest immediately struck the boy sharply on the cheek, and in a very gruff voice, shouted so that many people could hear, "Leave the altar and don't come back!" That boy became Tito, the Communist leader who ruled Yugoslavia for many decades.

One day in a large city cathedral, a young boy was serving a bishop at a Sunday Mass. He, too, accidentally dropped the cruet of wine. The bishop turned to him, but rather than responding in anger, he gently whispered with a warm twinkle in his eyes, "Someday you will be a priest." That boy grew up to become Archbishop Fulton Sheen.

Words have power. The childhood phrase, "Sticks and stones can break my bones, but words can never hurt me," simply isn't true. Words do hurt. They wound—sometimes deeply.

But words also can reward, build self-esteem, create friendships, give hope, and render a blessing. Words can heal and drive us to achieve great things.

Watch what you say to a friend today! Are your words like poison to the heart, or do they drip with the sweetness of honey?

217

LET EACH MAN THINK HIMSELF AN ACT OF GOD, HIS MIND A THOUGHT OF GOD, HIS LIFE A BREATH OF GOD.

God created people in his own image;
God patterned them after himself.
Genesis 1:27 NLT

218

A farmer once caught a young eagle in the forest, brought it home, and raised it among his ducks and turkeys. Five years later, a naturalist came to visit him and saw the bird. "That's an eagle, not a chicken!" he said. "Yes," said the farmer, "but I've raised it to be a chicken." "Still," said the naturalist, "it has a wing span of fifteen feet. It's an eagle!" "It will never fly," said the farmer. The naturalist disagreed, and they decided to put their argument to the test.

First, the naturalist picked up the eagle and said, "Eagle, thou art an eagle; thou dost belong to the sky and not to this earth; stretch forth thy wings and fly." The eagle saw the chickens and jumped down. The next day, the naturalist took the eagle to the top of the house and said the same thing before letting the eagle go. Again, it spotted the chickens below and fluttered down to join them in feeding.

"One more try," said the naturalist. He took the eagle up on a mountain. The trembling bird looked around, and then the naturalist made it look into the sun. Suddenly, the eagle stretched out its wings, gave a mighty screech, and flew away, never to return.

People may say you are just a hunk of flesh—a chicken rather than an eagle. But deep inside, you have a spirit created in God's image, and you are destined to fly.

REALLY GREAT MEN
AND WOMEN ARE
THOSE WHO ARE
NATURAL, FRANK,
AND HONEST WITH
EVERYONE WITH
WHOM THEY COME
INTO CONTACT.

Don't show favoritism.
James 2:1 NIV

220

In ancient Greece, the philosopher Aristippus—considered by all who knew him to be the master of political craftiness—learned to get along well in royal circles by flattering the tyrant Denys. Not only did he flatter Denys, but he was proud that he did. In fact, Aristippus disdained less prosperous fellow philosophers and wise men who refused to stoop that low.

One day Aristippus saw his colleague Diogenes washing vegetables, and said to him, "If you would only learn to flatter King Denys, you would not have to be washing lentils." Diogenes looked up slowly and replied, "And you, if you had only learned to live on lentils, would not have to flatter King Denys."

Another way to regard flattery is this:

F—foolish
L—laughable
A—accolades
T—to
T—tell
E—everyone
R—'round
Y—you

Speak the truth sincerely. When the truth is painful, consider the option of remaining silent!

221

'TIS BETTER TO BE ALONE THAN IN BAD COMPANY.

Do not be misled: "Bad company
corrupts good character."
1 Corinthians 15:33 NIV

Coach Gregory watched with pride as Rashaan Salaam accepted the Heisman Trophy. He recalled the hotshot eighteen-year-old who, finally free from his mother's tight discipline, had arrived in Colorado ready to devour the world. He said, "Rashaan was a gangster wannabe. He came here wearing all this red stuff, talking about gangs. He hadn't done it back home because his mother would never have tolerated it." And neither did Gregory. He never lectured or preached to Rashaan, but he did ask him questions.

When Rashaan came to him talking about his new friends, Gregory said, "Sure, they are your friends, but are you their friend? They know what you're trying to accomplish. They know the potential you have to do great things. If you are their friend, when they get ready to get into something, they'll say, 'Salaam, get out of here. Go home and study.'"

As a coach, Gregory wanted Salaam to "find daylight" and get into the end zone, but as his friend, he wanted him to live in the daylight and reach life's goal line as a productive citizen.

Winning a football game is never a one-man effort. It's a team effort. The same holds true for life, and the good news is you can choose the players on your team!

THE ROTTEN APPLE SPOILS HIS COMPANION.

He that walketh with wise men shall be wise:
but a companion of fools shall be destroyed.
Proverbs 13:20

In his book, *The Mind of Watergate,* psychiatrist Leo Rangell, M.D., relates what he calls a "compromise of integrity" as he analyzes the relationship between former President Richard M. Nixon and several of his closest confidants. He records a conversation between investigative committee member Senator Howard Baker and young Herbert L. Porter:

Baker: "Did you ever have qualms about what you were doing? Did you ever think of saying, 'I don't think this is quite right.' Did you ever think of that?"

Porter: "Yes, I did."

Baker: "What did you do about it?"

Porter: "I didn't do anything."

Baker: "Why didn't you?"

Porter: "In all honesty, probably because of the fear of group pressure that would ensue, I was afraid of not being considered a team player."

There's nothing wrong with being a team player, as long as you choose the right team! You will become like your friends, even as they change and become a little more like you. Therefore, choose your friends cautiously and thoughtfully.

PATIENCE IS BITTER BUT ITS FRUIT IS SWEET.

Ye have need of patience, that,
after ye have done the will of God,
ye might receive the promise.
Hebrews 10:36

CLASS OF
2001

We often think of great artists and musicians as having "bursts" of genius. More often, they are models of painstaking patience. Their greatest works tend to have been accomplished over long periods and in extreme hardships.

- Beethoven is said to have rewritten each bar of his music at least a dozen times.

- Josef Haydn produced more than eight hundred musical compositions before writing *The Creation,* the oratorio for which he is most famous.

- Michelangelo's *Last Judgment* is considered one of the twelve master paintings of the ages. It took him eight years to complete. He produced more than two thousand sketches and renderings in the process.

- Leonardo da Vinci worked on *The Last Supper* for ten years, often working so diligently that he would forget to eat.

When he was quite elderly, the pianist Ignace Paderewski was asked by an admirer, "Is it true that you still practice every day?" He replied, "Yes, at least six hours a day." The admirer said in awe, "You must have a world of patience." Paderewski said, "I have no more patience than the next fellow. I just use mine."

Put your patience to use in the pursuit of your dreams.

SOME MEN DREAM OF WORTHY ACCOMPLISHMENTS, WHILE OTHERS STAY AWAKE AND DO THEM.

Whatever you do, work at it with all your heart,
as working for the Lord, not for men.
Colossians 3:23 NIV

In 1972 *Life* magazine published a story about the amazing adventures of John Goddard. When he was fifteen, John's grandmother said, "If only I had done that when I was young." Determined not to have to make that statement at the end of his life, John wrote out one hundred and twenty-seven goals for his life.

He named ten rivers he wanted to explore and seventeen mountains he wanted to climb. He determined to become an Eagle Scout, a world traveler, and a pilot. Also on his list was: ride a horse in the Rose Bowl parade, dive in a submarine, retrace the travels of Marco Polo, read the Bible from cover to cover, and read the entire *Encyclopedia Britannica*.

He also planned to read the entire works of Shakespeare, Plato, Dickens, Socrates, Aristotle, and several other classic authors. He desired to learn to play the flute and violin, marry, have children (he had five), pursue a career in medicine, and serve as a missionary for his church.

Sound impossible? At the age of forty-seven, John Goddard had accomplished one hundred and three of his goals!

What goals have you set for your life? Write them down, memorize them, meditate on them, pursue them. Just dreaming will get you nowhere. Dreaming, setting goals, and actively working to accomplish those goals will make your dreams a reality.

THE GREAT TEST OF A MAN'S CHARACTER IS HIS TONGUE.

Self-control means controlling the tongue!
A quick retort can ruin everything.
Proverbs 13:3 TLB

230

William Penn, founding leader of the colony that became Pennsylvania, had these rules for conversation:

- "Avoid company where it is not profitable or necessary, and in those occasions, speak little, and last.
- Silence is wisdom where speaking is folly, and always safe.
- Some are so foolish as to interrupt and anticipate those that speak instead of hearing and thinking before they answer, which is uncivil, as well as silly.
- If thou thinkest twice before thou speakest once, thou wilt speak twice the better for it.
- Better to say nothing than not to the purpose. And to speak pertinently, consider both what is fit and when it is fit to speak.
- In all debates, let truth be thy aim, not victory or an unjust interest; and endeavor to gain, rather than to expose, thy antagonist."

Though few achieve it, one of the greatest skills you can develop in life is the ability to control your tongue! It is an invaluable asset in every area of life. Yet many people never appreciate its worth. How about you?

CLASS OF 2001

231

SCHOOL SEEKS TO GET YOU READY FOR EXAMINATIONS; LIFE GIVES THE FINALS.

Examine yourselves to see whether you are in the faith; test yourselves.
2 Corinthians 13:5 NIV

CLASS OF 2001

The Koh-in-noor diamond is among the world's most spectacular. It is part of the British crown jewels, presented to Queen Victoria by a maharajah in India when the maharajah was only a young boy.

Years later, when he was a grown man, the maharajah visited Queen Victoria in England. He asked that the stone be brought from the Tower of London, where it was kept in safety, to Buckingham Palace. The queen did as he requested.

Taking the diamond in his hand, he knelt before the queen and presented it back to her, saying, "Your Majesty, I gave this jewel when I was a child, too young to know what I was doing. I want to give it to you again in the fullness of my strength, with all of my heart and affection and gratitude, now and forever, fully realizing all that I do."

A day will come when you likely will look back and say, "I'm grateful for my teachers, and the lessons they taught me about discipline, concentration, hard work, cooperation, and the right and wrong ways to compete." Even more valuable will be the day when you look in a mirror and say, "Knowing what I now know about life, I see value in continuing to teach these lessons to myself."

DILIGENCE IS THE MOTHER OF GOOD FORTUNE.

The plans of the diligent lead to profit.
Proverbs 21:5 NIV

CLASS OF 2001

The "Sixty-four Thousand-Dollar Question" was the hottest show on television in 1955. The more Joyce watched the program, the more she thought, "I could do that." At the time, Joyce had quit her teaching job to raise her daughter, and she and her husband were living on fifty dollars a month. She never dreamed of winning the top prize—*any* prize at that point would have helped greatly.

As a psychologist by training, Joyce analyzed the show. She saw that each contestant had a built-in incongruity—the marine who was a gourmet cook, the shoemaker who knew about opera. She looked at herself. She was a short, blond psychologist and mother with no incongruity. After some thought, she decided to become an expert in boxing! She ate, drank, and slept boxing, studying its statistics, personalities, and history. When she felt she was ready, she applied as a contestant for the show, was accepted, won, and won again, until she eventually won the sixty-four thousand-dollar prize.

That experience led her to dream of a career as a television journalist who could translate the results of psychological research into terms that people could use in their everyday lives. Once she saw that possibility, there was no stopping Dr. Joyce Brothers.

True success never comes by chance. Diligently apply yourself to your goals, and your dreams will come true.

THE ROAD TO SUCCESS IS DOTTED WITH MANY TEMPTING PARKING PLACES.

Let us lay aside every weight, and the sin which doth so easily beset us, and let us run with patience the race that is set before us.

Hebrews 12:1

CLASS OF 2001

The first thing to emerge at a baby giraffe's birth is its front hooves and head. Minutes later, the newborn is hurled from its mother's body, falls ten feet, and lands on its back. Within seconds, it rolls to an upright position with its legs tucked under its body. From this position, it views the world for the first time and shakes off any remaining birthing fluid.

The mother giraffe lowers her head just long enough to take a quick look at her calf, and then she does what seems to be a very unreasonable thing—she kicks her baby, sending it sprawling head over heels. If it doesn't get up, she kicks it again and again until the calf finally stands on its wobbly legs. Then what does the mother giraffe do? She kicks it off its feet! Why? She wants it to remember how to get up.

In the wild, baby giraffes must be able to get up as quickly as possible to stay with the herd and avoid becoming a meal for lions, hyenas, leopards, or wild dogs. The best way a mother giraffe has of ensuring her calf's safety is to teach it to get up quickly.

Don't complain if those who love you push you into action when you'd rather be in "park." They are doing you a favor.

237

WHEN YOU ARE LABORING FOR OTHERS, LET IT BE WITH THE SAME ZEAL AS IF IT WERE LABORING FOR YOURSELF.

Each of you should look not only to your own interests, but also to the interests of others.
Philippians 2:4 NIV

On May 21, 1946, a scientist at Los Alamos was carrying out a necessary experiment in preparation for an atomic test to be conducted in the waters of the South Pacific. He had successfully performed this experiment many times before. It involved pushing two hemispheres of uranium together to determine the amount of U-235 needed for a chain reaction—the amount scientists call "a critical mass." Just as the mass became critical, he would push the hemispheres apart with his screwdriver, instantly stopping the chain reaction.

That day, however, just as the material became critical, the screwdriver slipped. The hemispheres of uranium came too close together, and instantly, the room was filled with a dazzling bluish haze. Young Louis Soltin, instead of ducking and thereby possibly saving himself, tore the two hemispheres apart with his hands, thus interrupting the chain reaction.

In this instant, self-forgetful act, he saved the lives of seven other people who were in the room. He, however, died nine days later.

Today, do something for someone else with the same energy you would use if you were doing it for yourself.

THE BIBLE KNOWS
NOTHING OF A
HIERARCHY OF
LABOR. NO WORK
IS DEGRADING.
IT IF OUGHT TO
BE DONE, THEN IT
IS GOOD WORK.

To rejoice in his labour; this is the gift of God.
Ecclesiastes 5:19

CLASS OF
2001

When David was twelve, he convinced a restaurant manager that he was actually sixteen and was hired as a lunch-counter waiter for twenty-five cents an hour. The place was owned by two Greek immigrant brothers, Frank and George, who had started their lives in America as a dishwasher and hot-dog seller.

David remembers that Frank and George set high standards and never asked anything of their employees that they wouldn't do themselves. Frank once told David, "As long as you try, you can always work for me." Trying meant everything from working hard to treating customers politely. Once, when Frank noticed a waitress giving a customer a rough time, he fired her on the spot and waited on the table himself. David determined that would never happen to him.

The usual tip for waiters in those days was a dime, but David discovered that if he brought the food out quickly and was especially polite, he sometimes got a quarter as a tip. He set a goal for himself to see how many customers he could wait on in one night. His record was one hundred!

Today, R. David Thomas is better known as "Dave," the founder and senior chairman of Wendy's International, Inc., a chain of forty-three hundred restaurants.

No matter what job you do, do it well.

THE RIPEST PEACH IS HIGHEST ON THE TREE.

Let us not become weary in doing good,
for at the proper time we will reap
a harvest if we do not give up.
Galatians 6:9 NIV

242

McCormick's father was what many might call a "tinkerer." A mechanical genius, he invented many farm devices. Sadly, however, he became the laughing-stock of his community for attempting to make a grain-cutting device. For years, he worked on the project but never succeeded in getting it to operate reliably.

In spite of the discouragement his father experienced and the continuing ridicule of neighbors, young McCormick took up the old machine as his own project. He also withstood years of experimentation and failure. Then one day, he succeeded in constructing a reaper that would harvest grain.

Even so, jealous opposition prevented the invention from being used for a number of years. McCormick was able to make sales only after he gave a personal guarantee to each purchaser that the reaper would do the job he claimed it could do. Finally, after decades of trial and error, hoping and waiting, a firm in Cincinnati agreed to manufacture one hundred machines, and the famous McCormick reaper was born.

To get to the ripest peach on the highest branch, you need to climb one limb at a time and not be defeated by the scrape of bark, the occasional fall, and the frequent feeling of being left dangling!

243

WHEN YOU DO THE
THINGS YOU HAVE TO
DO WHEN YOU HAVE
TO DO THEM, THE DAY
WILL COME WHEN
YOU CAN DO THE
THINGS YOU WANT
TO DO WHEN YOU
WANT TO DO THEM.

He becometh poor that dealeth with a slack hand:
but the hand of the diligent maketh rich.
Proverbs 10:4

The bee is often described as busy. It deserves this adjective! To produce one pound of honey, a bee must visit fifty-six thousand clover heads. Since each head has sixty flower tubes, a bee must make a total of three million three hundred sixty thousand visits. In the process, the average bee would travel the equivalent of three times around the world.

To make just one *tablespoon* of honey, the amount that might go on a biscuit, a little bee must make forty-two hundred trips to the flowers, averaging about ten trips a day, each trip lasting approximately twenty minutes. It visits four hundred different flowers.

Day in, day out, the work of a bee is fairly unglamorous. It flies, it takes in nectar, it flies some more, and it deposits nectar. But in the process, it produces, and what it produces creates a place for it in the hive.

You may think your daily chores are a waste of time. But completing them is actually preparing you to succeed in life. One day you won't even have to think: *I must get disciplined. I must get to work. I must stick with it.* If you do your chores faithfully and to the best of your ability, the process will become a part of the way you tackle every challenge in life.

A MAN WITHOUT MIRTH IS LIKE A WAGON WITHOUT SPRINGS, HE IS JOLTED DISAGREEABLY BY EVERY PEBBLE IN THE ROAD.

A merry heart doeth good like a medicine:
but a broken spirit drieth the bones.
Proverbs 17:22

246

Dr. Ashley Montagu met two young men shortly after the end of World War II. They had spent two years in Auschwitz, the cruel death camp operated by the Nazis. Prior to Auschwitz, they had lived in Vienna in a cellar where they had been kept hidden by Christian friends. All of the others housed with them in the cellar had been exterminated solely because they were Jews.

After the war ended, these two men had walked from Vienna to Berlin, hoping to find relatives. There, they were picked up by an American Jewish soldier who brought them to America. Both of them wanted to become physicians, and that's how Dr. Montagu, a professor in a medical school, came to meet them. Noting that they "didn't exhibit any of the scars that one might have expected from their unhappy existence," he asked them how they came to be such cheerful people.

These two replied, "A group of us decided that no matter what happened, it wouldn't get us down." They told him they had attempted to be cheerful regardless of their circumstances, never yielding for a moment to the idea that they were either inferior or doomed.

They were living proof to Dr. Montagu that a positive mental attitude and a cheerful demeanor can help us survive even under impossible conditions.

THE TRUEST SELF-RESPECT IS NOT TO THINK OF SELF.

Don't be selfish. . . . Be humble,
thinking of others as better than yourself.
Philippians 2:3 TLB

CLASS OF 2001

Leonard Bernstein was once asked which instrument was the most difficult to play. He thought for a moment and said, "The second fiddle. I can get plenty of first violinists, but to find someone who can play the second fiddle with enthusiasm—that's a problem. And if we have no second fiddle, we have no harmony."

General Robert E. Lee knew the value of playing second fiddle. This great general never stopped being a true southern gentleman. Once, while riding on a train to Richmond, he was seated at the rear of the car. All the other places were filled with officers and soldiers. A poorly dressed, elderly woman boarded the coach at a rural station, and finding no seat offered to her, she trudged down the aisle toward the back of the car.

Immediately, Lee stood up and offered her his seat. The other men then arose one after another and offered the general his seat. "No, gentlemen," he replied, "if there are no seats for this lady, there can be none for me!"

Selfishness is a sign of insecurity. Humility and the ability to consider the needs of others first are signs of self-respect.

249

ONLY HE WHO CAN SEE THE INVISIBLE CAN DO THE IMPOSSIBLE.

By faith we understand that the entire universe was formed at God's command, that what we now see did not come from anything that can be seen.

Hebrews 11:3 NLT

A number of years ago the John Hancock Mutual Life Insurance Company ran an ad that said:

There was once a man who loved nature with such a deep and moving love that she told him one of her secrets. She gave him the power to create new plants. The man, whose name was Luther Burbank, saw that every plant was a child. It had its own face, own promise, its unique touch of genius or character. And if that promise were tended and encouraged, the plant would grow more useful and beautiful each year.

Luther Burbank made potatoes grow larger, whiter, more delicious than they had ever been. He taught the cactus of the desert to throw away its spines, so that cattle could fatten upon it, and made the blackberry shed its thorns, so it would not cut the fingers of the pickers. For him, the plum grew without pits, and strawberries ripened all year.

He left the earth covered with flowers and fruits that no one had ever attempted to grow before. And all because he knew a secret. He knew that everything that lives has the power to become greater.

Ask God to show you new possibilities. Put your mind to them. Let them be the focus of your thoughts, and then pursue them! You, too, can accomplish the impossible.

ALWAYS BEAR IN MIND THAT YOUR OWN RESOLUTION TO SUCCEED IS MORE IMPORTANT THAN ANY OTHER ONE THING.

The Lord GOD will help me; therefore shall I not be confounded: therefore have I set my face like a flint, and I know that I shall not be ashamed.
Isaiah 50:7

Famous stage and film actress Helen Hayes believed her "resoluteness" about her own potential for success played an important role at the beginning of her career. She once told the story of a particular audition:

> Before the authors gave me the script, they observed, in a matter-of-course manner, "Of course you play piano? You'll have to sing to your own accompaniment in the piece." As these alarming tidings were in the course of being made, I caught a bewildered look in my mother's eyes, and so I spoke up before she could. "Certainly I play piano," I answered.
>
> As we left the theater, my mother sighed, "I hate to see you start under a handicap," she said. "What made you say you could play piano?" "The feeling that I will play before rehearsals begin," I said. We went at once to try to rent a piano and ended by buying one. I began lessons at once, practiced finger exercises till I could no longer see the notes—and began rehearsals with the ability to accompany myself. Since then, I have never lived too far from a piano.

What you believe about your own potential for success counts far more than what any other person may believe. Believe what God believes about you—you were created for success.

TRIUMPH IS JUST "UMPH" ADDED TO TRY.

*Whatsoever thy hand findeth
to do, do it with thy might.
Ecclesiastes 9:10*

CLASS OF
2001

Many years ago in England, a small boy grew up speaking with a lisp. He was never a scholar in school. When war broke out involving his nation, he was rejected from service, and told "We need *men*." He once rose to address the House of Commons, and all present walked out of the room. In fact, he often spoke to empty chairs and echoes. But one day, he became Prime Minister of Great Britain, and with stirring speeches and bold decisions, he led his nation to victory.

His name was Sir Winston Churchill.

Many years ago in Illinois, a man with only a few years of formal education failed in business in '31, was defeated in a run for the state legislature in '32, again failed in business in '33, was elected to the legislature in '34, but defeated for speaker in '38. He was defeated for elector in '40, defeated for Congress in '43, elected to Congress in '46, but defeated in '48. He was defeated for Senate in '55, defeated for the vice-presidential nomination in '56, and defeated for the Senate in '58. But in 1860, he was elected president.

His name was Abraham Lincoln.

You cannot be defeated until you stop trying.

PERSEVERANCE CAN DO ANYTHING WHICH GENIUS CAN DO AND A GREAT MANY THINGS WHICH GENIUS CANNOT.

*The thoughts of the diligent
tend only to plenteousness.
Proverbs 21:5*

256

A young man in need of work once saw this advertisement in a Boston newspaper: "Wanted, young man as an understudy to a financial statistician, P.O. Box 1720." The young man decided this was just the kind of job he wanted, so he replied to the ad but received no answer. He wrote again, and even a third time with no reply. Next, he went to the Boston post office and asked for the name of the holder of Box 1720, but the clerk refused to give it, as did the postmaster.

Early one morning, an idea came to the young man. He rose early, took the first train to Boston, went to the post office, and stood watch near Box 1720. After awhile, a man appeared, opened the box, and took out the mail. The young man followed him as he returned to the office of a stock brokerage firm. The young man entered and asked for the manager.

In the interview, the manager asked, "How did you find out that I was the advertiser?" The young man told about his detective work, to which the manager replied, "Young man, you are just the kind of persistent fellow I want. You are employed!"

Don't let a few setbacks stop you from pursuing your goals in life! Many people can't unlock the door to their dreams because they don't take enough time to locate the key.

I THINK THE ONE LESSON I HAVE LEARNED IS THAT THERE IS NO SUBSTITUTE FOR PAYING ATTENTION.

We ought to give the more earnest heed to the things which we have heard, lest at any time we should let them slip.
Hebrews 2:1

258

Henry P. Davison was a prominent American financier and one-time head of the American Red Cross. From poor beginnings, he worked his way up the ladder until he became the president of a large New York City bank.

While he was a cashier of that bank, a would-be robber came to his window, pointed a revolver at him, and passed a check across his window counter. The check was for one million dollars, payable to the Almighty. Davison remained calm, even though he realized the gravity of the situation. In a loud voice, he repeated the words on the check back to the person standing in front of him, emphasizing the "million dollars."

Then Davison graciously asked the would-be robber how he would like the million dollars for the Almighty. He then proceeded to count out small bills. In the meantime, the suspicion of a guard had been aroused by the strange request he had overheard. He disarmed the robber and prevented the theft.

In later years, Davison was known to advise those who asked, that courtesy, readiness, willingness, and alertness accomplish more for a person than simply being smart.

It has been said that one of the skills of a good communicator is the ability to listen. Paying attention to the words and actions of those around you may be the best schooling you'll ever receive.

259

A GOOD LISTENER IS NOT ONLY POPULAR EVERYWHERE, BUT AFTER A WHILE HE KNOWS SOMETHING.

The ear that heareth the reproof
of life abideth among the wise.
Proverbs 15:31

CLASS OF
2001

An American Indian was once visiting New York City, and as he walked the busy Manhattan streets with a friend from the city, he suddenly stopped, tilted his head to one side, and said, "I hear a cricket."

"You're crazy," his friend said. The Cherokee answered, "No, I hear a cricket. I do! I'm sure of it."

The friend replied, "It's the noon hour. People are jammed on the sidewalks, cars are honking, taxis are whizzing by, the city is full of noise. And you think you can hear a cricket?"

"I'm sure I do," said the visitor. He listened even more closely and then walked to the corner, spotted a shrub in a large cement planter, dug into the leaves underneath it, and pulled out a cricket. His friend was astounded.

The man said, "It all depends on what your ears have been tuned to hear, my friend. Let me show you." The Cherokee reached into his pocket, pulled out a handful of loose change, and dropped the coins on the pavement. Every head within a half block turned. "See what I mean?" he said, picking up the coins. "It all depends on what you are listening for."

Listen today to those things that will make you wise.

YOU MAY BE DISAPPOINTED IF YOU FAIL, BUT YOU ARE DOOMED IF YOU DON'T TRY.

The sluggard craves and gets nothing, but the desires of the diligent are fully satisfied.
Proverbs 13:4 NIV

These words were spelled out in lights at the eighteenth Olympics in Tokyo: "The most important thing in the Olympic Games is not to win but to take part; just as the most important thing in life is not the triumph but the struggle. The essential thing is to have fought well."

The athletes who make it to the Olympic games are already the best of the best from each nation. Each athlete has excelled in ways few of his or her peers will ever reach. Yet only one will wear a gold medal, one a silver, and one a bronze.

Those who are so accustomed to winning, face the devastating possibility of losing before not only their teammates, but also their countrymen, and in this age of worldwide television, before the entire world. How vital it is for these athletes to keep their perspective—that winning is not the important issue at the Olympics but the opportunity to compete, to try, and to give one's best effort.

Regardless of the arena in which you compete, winning is not what is truly important. Trying and giving your best effort is what molds within you the lasting traits and character that are "better than gold."

SUCCESS IS NEVER FINAL; FAILURE IS NEVER FATAL; IT IS COURAGE THAT COUNTS.

Be of good courage, and he shall strengthen
your heart, all ye that hope in the LORD.
Psalm 31:24

In *The Seven habits of Highly Effective People,* Stephen R. Covey writes:

> One of the most inspiring times Sandra and I have ever had took place over a four-year period with a dear friend of ours named Carol, who had a wasting cancer disease. She had been one of Sandra's bridesmaids, and they had been best friends for more than twenty-five years.
>
> When Carol was in the very last stages of the disease, Sandra spent time at her bedside helping her write her personal history. She returned from those protracted and difficult sessions almost transfixed by admiration for her friend's courage and her desire to write special messages to be given to her children at different stages in their lives.
>
> Carol would take as little pain medication as possible, so that she would have full use of her mental and emotional faculties. Then she would whisper into a tape recorder or directly to Sandra. Carol was so proactive, so brave, and so concerned about others that she became an enormous source of inspiration to many people around her.

In today's world, courage is a desperately needed trait. Seek to develop it.

WHEN YOUR WORK SPEAKS FOR ITSELF, DON'T INTERRUPT.

Be sure to do what you should, for then you will enjoy the personal satisfaction of having done your work well, and you won't need to compare yourself to anyone else.

Galatians 6:4 NLT

CLASS OF 2001

A quiet forest dweller who lived high above an Austrian village in the Alps was hired by a town council to keep the pristine mountain springs—the source of the town's water supply—clear of debris. With faithful regularity, the old man patrolled the hills; clearing away silt and removing leaves and branches from the springs.

Over time, the village became prosperous. Mill wheels turned, farms were irrigated, and tourists came. Years passed. Then at a council meeting about the city budget, a member noticed the salary figure for the old man. He asked, "Who is he and why do we keep him on the payroll? Has anybody seen him? For all we know, he might be dead." The council voted to dispense with his services.

For several weeks nothing changed. Then the trees began to shed their leaves. One afternoon, a town citizen noticed a brown tint to the water. Within another week, slick covered sections of the canals, and a foul odor was detected. Sickness broke out.

The town council called a special meeting, and reversing their error in judgment, rehired the old man. Renewed life soon returned to the village as the sparkling waters returned.

Not everyone's job will make the six o'clock news everyday, but no matter where God places you, do your work unto Him, and He will reward you for your faithfulness.

POOR EYES LIMIT YOUR SIGHT. POOR VISION LIMITS YOUR DEEDS.

Where there is no vision, the people perish.
Proverbs 29:18

One of the great disasters of history took place in 1271. In that year, Niccolo and Matteo Polo, the father and uncle of Marco Polo, visited Kubla Khan, who was considered the world ruler, with authority over all China, all India, and all of the East.

The Kubla Khan was attracted to the story of Christianity as Niccolo and Matteo told it to him. He said to them, "You shall go to your high priest and tell him on my behalf to send me a hundred men skilled in your religion, and I shall be baptized. And when I am baptized all my barons and great men will be baptized and their subjects will receive baptism, too. So there will be more Christians here than there are in your parts."

Nothing was done, however, in response to what the Kubla Khan had requested. After thirty years only a handful of missionaries were sent—too few too late.

The West apparently did not have the vision to see the East won to Christ. The mind boggles at the possible ways the world might be different today if thirteenth-century China, India, and the other areas of the Orient had been converted to Christianity.

If you lack vision today, ask God for it. He has wonders to reveal to you that you can't yet imagine!

CLASS OF 2001

269

PEOPLE ARE LONELY BECAUSE THEY BUILD WALLS INSTEAD OF BRIDGES.

You should be like one big happy family . . . loving one another with tender hearts and humble minds.
1 Peter 3:8 TLB

A fable is told of a young orphan boy who had no family and no one to love him. Feeling sad and lonely, he was walking through a meadow one day when he saw a small butterfly caught in a thorn bush. The more the butterfly struggled to free itself, the deeper the thorns cut into its fragile body. The boy carefully released the butterfly, but instead of flying away, the butterfly transformed into an angel right before his eyes.

The boy rubbed his eyes in disbelief as the angel said, "For your wonderful kindness, I will do whatever you would like." The little boy thought for a moment, and then said, "I want to be happy!" The angel replied, "Very well," and then leaned toward him, whispered in his ear, and vanished.

As the little boy grew up, there was no one in the land as happy as he. When people asked him the secret of his happiness, he would only smile and say, "I listened to an angel when I was a little boy."

On his deathbed, his neighbors rallied around him and asked him to divulge the key to his happiness. The old man finally told them: "The angel told me that everyone, no matter how secure they seemed, no matter how old or young, how rich or poor, had need of me."

You have something to give to everyone you come in contact with today. Build bridges instead of walls!

271

FORGIVENESS MEANS GIVING UP YOUR RIGHT TO PUNISH ANOTHER.

"When you stand praying, if you hold anything against anyone, forgive him, so that your Father in heaven may forgive you your sins."
Mark 11:25 NIV

272

Lloyd John Ogilvie wrote in *Let God Love You,*

The hardest time to be gentle is when we know we are right and someone else is obviously dead wrong. But the greatest temptation for most of us is when someone has failed us and has admitted it, and their destiny or happiness is in our hands. We hold the power to give or refuse a blessing.

Recently, a dear friend hurt me in both word and action. Each time we met, I almost enjoyed the leverage of being the offended one. His first overtures of restitution were resisted because of the gravity of the judgment I had made. He had taken a key idea I had shared with him in confidence and had developed it as his own before I had a chance to use it. The plagiarism of ideas had been coupled with the use of some of my written material, reproduced under his name. The most difficult thing was to surrender my indignation and work through my hurt.

Finally, the Lord got through to me. His word was clear, "Lloyd, why is it so important to you who gets the credit, just so long as my work gets done?" I gave up my right to be what only God could be as this man's judge, and as I did, the gentle attitude began to flow.

When we withhold forgiveness, it not only hurts the person we don't want to forgive, it hurts us. Our creativity and the joy of living are stifled. When we forgive, we release peace and restoration to the forgiven, and to ourselves.

UNITY CREATES STRENGTH.

Always keep yourselves united in the Holy Spirit,
and bind yourselves together with peace.
Ephesians 4:3 NLT

274

CLASS OF
2001

Many people today seem to go through their day with their "stingers out," ready to attack others or to defend their position at the slightest provocation. We all would do well, however, to consider the full nature of the bees we sometimes seem to emulate.

Bees readily feed each other; sometimes they will even feed a bee from a different colony. The worker bees feed the queen bee, who cannot feed herself. They feed the drones during their period of usefulness in the hive. They feed their young. They seem to enjoy this social act of mutual feeding.

Bees cluster together for warmth in cold weather and fan their wings to cool the hive in hot weather, thus working for one another's comfort.

When the time comes for bees to move to new quarters, scouts report back to the group, doing a dance very similar to the one used to report a find of honey. When enough scouts have confirmed the suitability of the new location, the bees appear to make a common decision, take wing, and migrate together—all at the same time—in what we call a swarm.

Only as a last-resort measure of self-defense do bees engage their stingers, and then, never against their fellow bees. We would do well to learn from them!

ABILITIES ARE LIKE TAX DEDUCTIONS— WE USE THEM OR WE LOSE THEM.

*God has given gifts to each of you from his
great variety of spiritual gifts. Manage them well
so that God's generosity can flow through you.*
1 Peter 4:10 NLT

Andrew Carnegie, considered to be one of the first to emphasize self-esteem and the potential for inner greatness, was famous for his ability to produce millionaires from among his employees. One day a reporter asked him, "How do you account for the fact you have forty-three millionaires working for you?"

Carnegie replied, "They weren't rich when they came. We work with people the same way you mine gold. You have to remove a lot of dirt before you find a small amount of gold."

Andrew Carnegie knew how to bring about change in people. He helped them realize their hidden treasure within, inspired them to develop it, and then watched with encouragement as their lives were transformed.

The philosopher and psychologist William James once said, "Compared to what we ought to be, we are only half awake. We are making use of only a small part of our physical and mental resources. Stating the thing broadly, the human individual thus lives far within his limits. He possesses powers of various sorts which he habitually fails to use."

In other words, most people only develop a fraction of their abilities. Go for a bigger percentage in *your* life. Find the gold within!

277

COURAGE IS RESISTANCE TO FEAR, MASTERY OF FEAR— NOT ABSENCE OF FEAR.

Yea, though I walk through the valley of the shadow of death, I will fear no evil: for thou art with me; thy rod and thy staff they comfort me.
Psalm 23:4

Several years ago, a well-known television circus developed an act involving Bengal tigers. The act was performed live before a large audience. One night, the tiger trainer went into the cage with several tigers, and the door was routinely locked behind him. Spotlights flooded the cage, and television cameras moved in close so the audience could see every detail as he skillfully put the tigers through their paces.

In the middle of the performance, the worst happened: the lights went out. For nearly thirty long seconds, the trainer was locked in with the tigers in the darkness. With their superb night vision, the tigers could see him, but he could not see them. Still, he survived. When the lights came back on, he calmly finished his performance.

When the trainer was asked how he felt, he admitted to feeling chilling fear at first, but then, he said he realized that even though he couldn't see the big cats, they didn't know he couldn't see them. "I just kept cracking my whip and talking to them until the lights came on," he said. "They never knew I couldn't see them as well as they could see me."

Keep talking back to the tigers of fear that seem to be stalking you.

PRAYER IS AN INVISIBLE TOOL THAT IS WIELDED IN A VISIBLE WORLD.

The weapons of our warfare are
not carnal, but mighty through God
to the pulling down of strong holds.
2 Corinthians 10:4

CLASS OF
2001

B oth a major thoroughfare in Tel Aviv and a bridge that spans the Jordan River are named in honor of Viscount Edmund Henry Hynman Allenby, a British soldier. As commander of the Egyptian Expeditionary Forces, he outwitted and defeated the Turks in Palestine in 1917 and 1918, conquering Jerusalem without ever firing a single gun.

As a British soldier, Allenby was noncommittal about the official British policies concerning the establishment of a Jewish national home, but he did have a deep understanding of the Jews' desire to dwell in Palestine. At a reception in London, he spoke of being a little boy kneeling to say his evening prayers and repeating with his childhood lisp the words his mother prayed: "And, O Lord, we would not forget Thine ancient people, Israel; hasten the day when Israel shall again be Thy people and shall be restored to Thy favor and to their land."

Allenby concluded, "I never knew then that God would give me the privilege of helping to answer my own childhood prayers."

What you pray today may well be part of tomorrow's work. The world you envision in prayer may well be the world in which you one day will live!

MONEY IS LIKE AN ARM OR LEG: USE IT OR LOSE IT.

"Sell your possessions and give to the poor. Provide purses for yourselves that will not wear out, a treasure in heaven that will not be exhausted, where no thief comes near and no moth destroys."

Luke 12:33 NIV

A strange memorial can be found in the Mount Hope Cemetery of Hiawatha, Kansas. John M. Davis, an orphan, developed a strong dislike for his wife's family and insisted that none of his fortune go to them. He also refused requests that he eventually bequeath his estate for a hospital desperately needed in the area.

Instead, after his wife died in 1930, Mr. Davis chose to invest in an elaborate tomb for himself and his wife. The tomb includes a number of statues depicting the couple at various stages of their lives. One statue is of Mr. Davis as a lonely man seated beside an empty chair. It is titled "the vacant chair." Another shows him placing a wreath in front of his wife's tombstone. Many of the statues are made of Kansas granite. No money was left for the memorial's upkeep.

Today, largely because of its weight, this costly memorial is slowly sinking into the ground. It has become weathered and worn from the strong winds in this plains state. The townspeople regard the Davis tomb as an "old man's folly," and many predict that within the next fifty years, the memorial will have become obliterated beyond recognition and will need to be demolished. What could have been a living legacy will eventually become granite dust.

The Bible encourages us many times not to hoard up money to be used for our own selfish desires, but to be kind to the poor. When we do so, God blesses us with more. The more we give, the more we receive, and our legacy will last well into the future instead of sinking into oblivion.

IN TRYING TIMES, DON'T QUIT TRYING.

The righteous also shall hold on his way, and he that hath clean hands shall be stronger and stronger.

Job 17:9

In 1894, a sixteen-year-old boy found this note from his rhetoric teacher at Harrow, in England, attached to his report card: "A conspicuous lack of success." The young man kept on trying and went on to become one of the most famous speakers of the twentieth century. His name was Winston Churchill.

In 1902, an aspiring twenty-eight-year-old writer received a rejection letter from the poetry editor of *The Atlantic Monthly*. Returned, with a batch of poems he had sent, was this curt note: "Our magazine has no room for your vigorous verse." He kept on trying, however, and went on to see his work published. The poet's name was Robert Frost.

In 1905, the University of Bern turned down a Ph.D. dissertation as being fanciful and irrelevant. The young physics student who wrote the dissertation, kept on trying and went on to develop some of his ideas into widely accepted theories. His name was Albert Einstein.

When rejection shakes your resolve and dims your goals, keep on trying. If you do not quit, one day, you will be living out your dreams!

CLASS OF 2001

LET US NOT SAY,
"EVERY MAN IS THE
ARCHITECT OF HIS
OWN FORTUNE;"
BUT LET US SAY,
"EVERY MAN IS THE
ARCHITECT OF HIS
OWN CHARACTER."

*Till I die I will not remove mine integrity from me.
My righteousness I hold fast, and will not let it go:
my heart shall not reproach me so long as I live.*

Job 27:5-6

286

When Chief Justice Charles Evans Hughes moved to Washington D.C., to take up his duties on the Supreme Court, he transferred his church membership letter to a Baptist church in the area.

It was customary for all new members in this church to come to the front of the sanctuary at the close of the worship service so they might be officially introduced and welcomed. The first person to be called forward that morning was Ah Sing, a Chinese laundryman who had moved to Washington from the West Coast. He took his place at the far side of the church. As the dozen or so others were called forward that day, they came to the front and stood on the opposite side of the church, leaving Ah Sing standing alone.

Finally Chief Justice Hughes was called forward, and he immediately made his way to the front and proceeded to stand next to Ah Sing.

Your character is shown in many ways, but one of the most obvious is the way you treat people. You will grow in character and reputation if you treat others with kindness.

IT IS IMPOSSIBLE FOR THAT MAN TO DESPAIR WHO REMEMBERS THAT HIS HELPER IS OMNIPOTENT.

I will lift up my eyes to the mountains;
From where shall my help come?
My help comes from the LORD,
Who made heaven and earth.
Psalm 121:1-2 NAS

E. Stanley Jones tells the story of a missionary who became lost in an African jungle. Looking around, he saw nothing but bush and a few clearings. He stumbled about until he finally came across a native hut. He asked one of the natives if he could lead him out of the jungle and back to the mission station. The native agreed to help him.

"Thank you!" exclaimed the missionary. "Which way do I go?" The native replied, "Walk." And so they did, hacking their way through the unmarked jungle for more than an hour.

In pausing to rest, the missionary looked around and had the same overwhelming sense that he was lost. Again, all he could see was bush and a few clearings. "Are you quite sure this is the way?" he asked. "I don't see any path."

The native looked at him and replied, "Bwana, in this place there is no path. I am the path."

When we have no clues about which direction we're going, we must remember that God who guides us is omniscient—all-wise. When we feel alone, we must remember that God is omnipresent—always with us. When we are weak, we must remember that God is omnipotent—all-powerful. He is everything we need.

SERVICE IS NOTHING BUT LOVE IN WORK CLOTHES.

"The more lowly your service to others, the greater you are. To be the greatest, be a servant."
Matthew 23:11 TLB

L ord of all pots and pans and things,
Since I've no time to be
A saint by doing lovely things,
Or watching late with Thee,
Or dreaming in the dawnlight,
Or storming heaven's gates,
Make me a saint by getting meals,
And washing up the plates.
Although I have Martha's hands,
I have a Mary's mind;
And when I black the boots and shoes,
Thy sandals, Lord, I find.
I think of how they trod the earth,
Each time I scrub the floor.
Accept this meditation, Lord,
I haven't time for more.
Warm all the kitchen with Thy love,
And light it with Thy peace;
Forgive me all my worrying,
And make all grumbling cease.
Thou who didst love to give men food,
In a room or by the sea,
Accept this service that I do—
I do it unto Thee.

—Unknown

CLASS OF
2001

291

THOSE THAT HAVE DONE NOTHING IN LIFE ARE NOT QUALIFIED TO JUDGE THOSE THAT HAVE DONE LITTLE.

Judge not, and ye shall not be judged:
condemn not, and ye shall not be condemned.
Luke 6:37

God's Little Devotional Book

In the 1700s, an English cobbler kept a map of the world on his workshop wall so that he might be reminded to pray for the nations of the world. As the result of such prayer, he became especially burdened for a specific missionary outreach. He shared this burden at a meeting of ministers but was told by a senior minister, "Young man, sit down. When God wants to convert the heathen, He will do it without your help or mine."

The cobbler, William Carey, did not let this man's remarks put out the flame of his concern. When he couldn't find others to support the missionary cause that had burdened his soul, he became a missionary himself. His pioneering efforts in India are legendary; his mighty exploits for God are recorded by many church historians.

Be careful how you respond to the enthusiasm of others. Don't dampen someone's zeal for God. Be cautious in how you respond to the new ideas of another, that you don't squelch their God-given creativity.

Be generous and kind in evaluating the work of others so that you might encourage those things which are worthy. Be slow to judge and quick to praise. Then pray for the same in your own life!

PEOPLE, PLACES, AND THINGS WERE NEVER MEANT TO GIVE US LIFE. GOD ALONE IS THE AUTHOR OF A FULFILLING LIFE.

I am come that they might have life, and
that they might have it more abundantly.
John 10:10

A young man once came to Jesus asking Him what he needed to do to have eternal life. Jesus replied that he should keep the commandments. The young man then claimed that he had always kept them. Jesus advised, *If you want to be perfect, go, sell your possessions and give to the poor. . . . Then come, follow me* (Matthew 19:21 NIV).

The Scriptures tell us that the young man *went away sorrowful: for he had great possessions* (vs. 22). The young man not only had great possessions, but apparently those possessions had him! He couldn't bear to part with earthly, temporary goods in order to obtain heavenly, eternal goods. Jesus also taught, of course, that heaven's "wealth" can be ours now.

This young man didn't have to wait until he died to receive the benefits of eternal life. If he had been willing to give up his hold on his "stuff," he could have enjoyed great joy, peace, and fulfillment in life—things he was apparently lacking or he wouldn't have asked Jesus that particular question.

Take a look at your possessions today. Find those things you can give away to someone in need. Discover how rewarding giving can be!

ONE MAN WITH COURAGE MAKES A MAJORITY.

Be strong and of a good courage . . .
for the LORD thy God . . . will not
fail thee, nor forsake thee.
Deuteronomy 31:6

A teenager named Buck was walking to his father's apartment from a subway stop one day, when he suddenly realized that two men were flanking him.

"Give me your wallet," one of the men insisted. "I have a gun. Give me your wallet, or I'll shoot."

"No," Buck said.

"Hey, man, you don't understand. We're robbing you. Give me your wallet."

"No."

"Give me your wallet, or I'll knife you."

"No."

"Give me your wallet, or we'll beat you up."

By now the robber was *pleading* more than he was demanding.

"No," Buck said once again. He kept walking, and a few steps later, he realized that the two men had disappeared. As he related this story to a friend, the friend asked, "Weren't you scared?"

Buck replied, "Of course I was scared!"

"Then why didn't you give them your wallet?"

"Because," Buck answered matter-of-factly, "My learner's permit is in it."

While it may be wise to give in to the demands of a thief, the first and best answer to fear is always "No!"

YOU WILL NEVER MAKE A MORE IMPORTANT DECISION THAN THE PERSON YOU MARRY.

Therefore shall a man leave his father and his mother, and shall cleave unto his wife: and they shall be one flesh.
Genesis 2:24

When Ruth Bell was a teenager, she was sent from her childhood home in China to school in Korea. At the time, she fully intended to follow in her parents' footsteps and become a missionary. She envisioned herself a confirmed "old maid," ministering to the people of Tibet. While at school, however, Ruth did give some serious thought to the kind of husband that she *might* consider. As she tells in her book *A Time for Remembering,* she listed these particulars:

> If I marry: He must be so tall that when he is on his knees, as one has said, he reaches all the way to heaven. His shoulders must be broad enough to bear the burden of a family. His lips must be strong enough to smile, firm enough to say no, and tender enough to kiss. Love must be so deep that it takes its stand in Christ and so wide that it takes the whole lost world in. He must be active enough to save souls. He must be big enough to be gentle and great enough to be thoughtful. His arms must be strong enough to carry a little child.

Ruth Bell never did become a full-time missionary in Tibet. However, she did find a man worth marrying—Billy Graham. As his wife, Ruth Bell Graham became a missionary to the whole world!

It's crucial to marry the right person. Think about the qualities that you would like to have in a mate. If you haven't already, begin to pray for the person you will eventually marry. Even if you haven't met him or her yet, God knows who they are.

THE BIBLE HAS A WORD TO DESCRIBE "SAFE" SEX: IT'S CALLED MARRIAGE.

Marriage should be honored by all, and the marriage bed kept pure, for God will judge the adulterer and all the sexually immoral.
Hebrews 13:4 NIV

The 1960s were known for many rebellions, among them the sexual revolution. "Free love" spilled from the hippie movement into the mainstream American culture. Premarital sexual relations sanctioned by the "new morality" became openly flaunted.

One of the unexpected results of this trend, however, received little publicity. As reported by Dr. Francis Braceland, past president of the American Psychiatric Association and editor of the *American Journal of Psychiatry,* an increasing number of young people were admitted to mental hospitals during that time. In discussing this finding at a National Methodist Convocation of medicine and Theology, Braceland concluded, "A more lenient attitude on campus about premarital sexual experience has imposed stresses on some college women severe enough to cause emotional breakdown."

Looking back over the years since the "new morality" was sanctioned by a high percentage of the American culture, one finds a rising number of rapes, abortions, divorces, premarital pregnancies, single-family homes, and cases of sexually transmitted diseases, including herpes and HIV.

The evidence is compelling: the old morality produced safer, healthier, and happier people!

CLASS OF
2001

301

POLITENESS GOES FAR, YET COSTS NOTHING.

*"Treat others the same way
you want them to treat you."*
Luke 6:31 NAS

We often refer to courtesy as "common courtesy," but it is far from common these days.

A father once remarked about his three children: "My children may not be the brightest children in their class. They may not be the most talented or the most skilled. They may not achieve great fame, or earn millions of dollars. But by my insisting that they have good manners, I know they will be welcome in all places and by all people." How true!

Good manners—exhibiting common courtesies—are like a calling card. They open doors that are otherwise shut to those who are rude, crude, or unmannerly. They bring welcome invitations, and quite often, return engagements. They cover a multitude of weaknesses and flaws. They make other people feel good about themselves, and they in turn, extend kindness and generosity that might not otherwise be exhibited.

Good manners are a prerequisite for good friendships, good business associations, and good marriages—an important key to success!

CLASS OF 2001

SAY "THANK YOU" WHEN YOU RECEIVE A FAVOR, AND "EXCUSE ME" OR "PARDON ME" WHEN NEEDING TO INTERRUPT A DISCUSSION.

*While we have opportunity,
let us do good to all people.
Galatians 6:10 NAS*

Which virtuous behaviors on earth will still be required in Heaven?

• Courage? No. There will be nothing to fear in Heaven.

• Hope? No. We will have all that we desire.

• Faith? No. We will be in the presence of the Source of our faith, and all those things for which we have believed will have their fulfillment in Him and by His hand.

• Acts of charity toward those in need? No. There will be no hunger, thirst, nakedness, or homelessness in Heaven. All needs will be supplied.

• Sympathy? No, for there will be no more tears and no more pain.

• Courtesy? Yes! There will still be room for the exercise of courtesy—the kind greeting, the simple manners that offend no one but ease the way of all.

Good manners are important. They put people at ease, which in turn makes them more cooperative and happy.

Immanuel Kant once said, "Always treat a human being as a person, that is, as an end in himself, and not merely as a means to your end." Strive to impart dignity and self-worth to all you meet. Consider it dress rehearsal for your future life in Heaven!

305

KNOCK AND ASK PERMISSION BEFORE ENTERING SOMEONE'S ROOM.

Show respect for everyone.
1 Peter 2:17 NLT

CLASS OF
2001

A mother watched with raised eyebrows as her two sons took a hammer and a few nails from the kitchen utility drawer and scurried to one of the boys' rooms, giggling and talking in low voices. When she didn't hear any hammering, she continued with her chores. Then from the kitchen window, she saw one of the boys take a step-ladder from the garage. He disappeared from sight before she could call to him. A few minutes later her other son came into the kitchen to ask if she had any rope.

"No, what's going on?" Mom said. Her son said, "Nothin'." Mom pressed, "Are you sure?" but her son was out of sight.

Suspicious, Mom went to her son's room and found the door closed and locked. She knocked.

"What are you boys doing in there?" she asked. One son replied, "Nothin'."

Suspecting great mischief, she demanded entrance. "I want you to open this door right now!" she said. A few seconds later, the door popped open, and her son shouted, "Surprise!" as he handed her a rather crudely wrapped present. "Happy birthday, Mom!" the other boy added. Truly surprised, the mother stammered, "But what about the hammer, nails, ladder, and rope?" The boys grinned, "Oh Mom, those were just decoys."

YIELD TO THOSE IN AUTHORITY.

*Pray this way for kings and all others
who are in authority, so that we can live in
peace and quietness, in godliness and dignity.*
1 Timothy 2:2 NLT

CLASS OF
2001

While driving down a country road, a man came to a very narrow bridge. In front of the bridge, there was a sign that read, "Yield." Seeing no oncoming cars, the man continued across the bridge to his destination. On his way back, the man came to the same one-lane bridge, now from the opposite direction. To his surprise, he saw another "Yield" sign posted there.

Curious, he thought, *I'm sure there was one positioned on the other side.* Sure enough, when he reached the other side of the bridge and looked back, he saw the sign. Yield signs had been placed at both ends of the bridge, obviously with the intent that drivers from both directions were requested to give each other the right-of-way. It was a reasonable and doubly sure way to prevent a head-on collision.

If you find yourself in a combative situation with someone in authority, it is always wise to yield to them. If they have authority over you, a lack of respect will put you in a position to be punished or reprimanded. If you are of equal authority, an exercise of your power will only build resentment in a person better kept as an ally.

God's Little Devotional Book

RSVP PROMPTLY WHEN YOU RECEIVE AN INVITATION.

*Make the most of every
opportunity for doing good.*
Ephesians 5:16 NLT

The letters RSVP stand for the French phrase *responde vous s'il vous plait,* which means "please respond." This phrase on an invitation asks that you let the host or hostess know whether you plan to attend the function or not.

Occasionally, a handwritten invitation will say, "RSVP, regrets only." In this case, you are expected to notify the host only if you will *not* be attending. However, a truly thoughtful guest who plans to attend will still call or mail a note to the host to say thank you for the invitation and confirm that he or she will be attending.

Imagine that you planned a catered party for fifty guests and you were paying twenty-five dollars per guest. Then imagine that half your guests failed to respond, and ten of them did not show up. You would be spending two hundred and fifty dollars for people who simply were not considerate enough to let you know they would not be present. Would you consider those people to be thoughtful friends?

Be the kind of guest that you would like to have attend your own fanciest party!

RETURN WHAT YOU BORROW, ON TIME AND IN GOOD CONDITION.

Don't act thoughtlessly, but try to understand what the Lord wants you to do.
Ephesians 5:17 NLT

CLASS OF 2001

God's Little Devotional Book

A store once had the following lay-away policy: "We hold it in the store while you pay for it. You're mad. You take it from the store, and you don't pay for it. We're mad. Better that you're mad."

Mark Twain's neighbor may have had this policy in mind when Twain asked to borrow a certain book he had spotted in his neighbor's library. "Why, yes, Mr. Clemens, you're more than welcome to it," the neighbor said. "But I must ask you to read it here. You know I make it a rule never to let any book go out of my library."

Several days later, the neighbor came to Twain's house and asked if he could borrow his lawn mower since his had been taken to the repair shop. "Why, certainly," the humorist replied. "You're more than welcome to it. But I must ask you to use it only in my yard. You know I make it a rule."

Treat what you borrow as if it were a prized possession, returning it promptly. If something happens to it while it is in your possession, make repairs or replace it, not to your satisfaction but to the satisfaction of the owner. Always remember, even though the item is in your hands, it is not yours. It still belongs to the other person.

BE ON TIME FOR APPOINTMENTS; LEAVE ON TIME, TOO, FOR NOTHING IS MORE BORING THAN SOMEONE WHO OVERSTAYS HIS WELCOME.

Don't think only about your own affairs, but be interested in others, too, and what they are doing.
Philippians 2:4 NLT

314

Mr. Brown was in his final year of seminary, preparing to become a pastor. The policy of his school called for him to be available at a moment's notice to fill in for local churches that might need a preacher. Mr. Brown eagerly awaited such an opportunity, and at long last, his moment arrived. The pastor of a country church was called away on an emergency, and Mr. Brown was asked to fill the pulpit.

Having waited so long for the opportunity, and having so much to say, Mr. Brown soon became completely immersed in his own words. The more he preached, the more he became inspired to preach. When he glanced at his watch, he was shocked to see that he had preached for a full hour. He was truly embarrassed since he had been allotted only thirty minutes to preach. Knowing that he had preached well into the lunch hour, he made a heartfelt apology to the congregation and sat down.

A young woman hurried to him after the service ended. Obviously more impressed with his personality and appearance—and perhaps his availability—than she was with his message, she gushed, "Oh, Brother Brown, you needn't have apologized. You really didn't talk long—it just seemed long."

The old rule of thumb is, "Always leave them wanting more."

315

WHEN YOU WERE
BORN, YOU CRIED AND
THE WORLD REJOICED.
LIVE YOUR LIFE IN
SUCH A MANNER THAT
WHEN YOU DIE THE
WORLD CRIES AND
YOU REJOICE.

The memory of the righteous will be a blessing.
Proverbs 10:7 NIV

CLASS OF
2001

A painting in an ancient temple depicts a king forging a chain from his crown, while nearby, another scene shows a slave converting his chain into a crown. Underneath the painting is this inscription: "Life is what one makes it, no matter of what it is made."

You may have been born with certain "ingredients," just as a baker may find the staples of flour, sugar, and oil in his or her kitchen, but what you create from the talents and abilities God has given you is up to you! Live your life so that it might be measured according to these words of an anonymous poet:

> Not—How did he die? But—How did he live?
> Not—What did he gain? But—What did he give?
> These are the units to measure the worth
> Of a man as a man, regardless of birth.
> Not—What was his station? But—Had he a heart?
> And—How did he play his God-given part?
> Was he ever ready with a word of good cheer,
> To bring back a smile, to banish a tear?
> Not—What was his shrine? Nor—What was his creed?
> But—Had he befriended those really in need?
> Not—What did the sketch in the newspaper say?
> But—How many were sorry when he passed away?

ENDNOTES

1. *The Joy of Publishing,* Nat G. Bodian, (Open Horizons Publishing Company, Fairfield, IA, 1996), pp. 49-51.

2. *Jokes and Anecdotes,* edited by Joe Claro (Random House, New York, 1996), p. 163.

3. Rewrite of Internet story from *goodstories.com,* attributed to *The Church Humor Digest,* (Castle Books, Memphis,).

4. *The Holocaust Heroes,* David K. Fremon, (Enslow Publishers, Inc. Springfield, NJ, 1998), pp. 58-64.

5. *The Joy of Publishing,* Nat G. Bodian, (Open Horizons Publishing Co., Fairfield, IA, 1996), p. 124.

6. *Reader's Digest,* May, 1994, p. 114.

ACKNOWLEDGMENTS

We acknowledge and thank the following people for the quotes used in this book: Abraham Lincoln (10, 252), Les Brown (12), H. E. Jansen (14), John D. Rockefeller Jr. (16), Comte Georges-Louis Leclerc De Buffon (20), Harry Emerson Fosdick (22, 204), Ralph Waldo Emerson (24, 40), Daniel Webster (26), Charles Haddon Spurgeon (28, 108, 134), Phaedrus (32), Syrus (38, 200), Chuck Swindoll (44), Frank Borman (46), Ralph Washington Sockman (48), Josiah Gilbert Holland (50), Martha Washington (52), Sister Corita (54), Calvin Coolidge (56, 210), Sprat (62), Dr. Eugene Swearinger (64, 68), Thomas Jefferson (66, 126), Robert C. Edward (70), Andrew Jackson (72), Ed Cole (74, 86, 280), Woodrow Wilson (80, 132), John A. Shedd (82), Pablo Casals (88), Roy Disney (96), Helen Keller (98), Seneca (100), Aristotle (102, 162), Dwight L. Moody (104), William A. Ward (106), Moliere (110), Bob Bales (112), Charles C. Noble (114), Samuel Johnson (116, 292), Eleanor Roosevelt (118), John Skulley (120), George Bernard Shaw (122), Oprah Winfrey (124), Benjamin Franklin (130, 224), Terence (138), Henry Wadsworth Longfellow (144), Josh Billings (148), Jean Paul Richter (152), William James (154), Samuel Butler (156), H. P. Liddon (158), George Elliott (160), John R. Rice (164), William H. Danforth (166, 186, 220), Thomas Edison (168), Dwight Moody (170), George Edward Woodberry (172), Ronald E. Osborn (174), Bill Cosby (176), Winston Churchill (178, 264), Thomas Carlyle (182), Bacon (184), Lillian Dickson (188), Denis Diderot (190), Earl Nightingale (192), Horace (194), Louis D. Brandeis (196), Hannah More (198), Orlando A. Bri (202), Victor Hugo (206), David Dunn (208), Mark Twain (212, 278), Roy L. Smith (214), George Herbert (216), Philip James Bailey (218), George Washington (222), Oswald Chambers (230), Say (232), Cervantes (234), Ben Patterson (240), James Whitcomb Riley (242), Zig Ziglar (244), Henry Ward Beecher (246, 248, 256), Frank Gaines (250), Diane Sawyer (258), Wilson Mizner (260), Beverly Sills (262), Henry J. Kaiser (266), Franklin Field (268), Joseph Newton (270), Dennis Rainey (272), Henry Ford (282), George Dana Boardman (286), Jeremy Taylor (288), Gary Smalley and John Trent (294, 300), Dr. Eugene Swearingen (298), Samuel Smiles (302).

Additional copies of this book and other
titles in the *God's Little Devotional Book* series
are available from your local bookstore.

God's Little Devotional Book
God's Little Devotional Book for Students
God's Little Devotional Book for Graduates
God's Little Devotional Book for Dads
God's Little Devotional Book for Moms
God's Little Devotional Book for Men
God's Little Devotional Book for Couples
God's Little Devotional Book for Teens
God's Little Devotional Book for the Class of 2000

If you have enjoyed this book, or if it has impacted your life,
we would like to hear from you.

Please contact us at:

Honor Books
Department E
P.O. Box 55388
Tulsa, Oklahoma 74155
Or by e-mail at info@honorbooks.com

Honor Books
Tulsa, Oklahoma